The Inconvenient Gospel

The Inconvenient Gospel

*A Southern Prophet Tackles
War, Wealth, Race, and Religion*

Clarence Jordan

Edited by Frederick L. Downing

Plough

Published by Plough Publishing House
Walden, New York
Robertsbridge, England
Elsmore, Australia
www.plough.com

Plough produces books, a quarterly magazine, and Plough.com to encourage people and help them put their faith into action. We believe Jesus can transform the world and that his teachings and example apply to all aspects of life. At the same time, we seek common ground with all people regardless of their creed.

Plough is the publishing house of the Bruderhof, an international Christian community. The Bruderhof is a fellowship of families and singles practicing radical discipleship in the spirit of the first church in Jerusalem (Acts 2 and 4). Members devote their entire lives to serving God, one another, and their neighbors. They renounce private property and share everything. To learn more about the Bruderhof's faith, history, and daily life, see Bruderhof.com. (Views expressed by Plough authors are their own and do not necessarily reflect the position of the Bruderhof.)

A catalog record for this book is available from the British Library.
Library of Congress Cataloging-in-Publication Data

Names: Jordan, Clarence, author. | Downing, Frederick L., editor.
Title: The inconvenient gospel : a southern prophet tackles war, wealth,
  race, and religion / Clarence Jordan ; edited by Frederick L. Downing.
Description: Walden : Plough Publishing House, 2022. | Series: Plough
  spiritual guides : backpack classics | Includes bibliographical
  references and index.
Identifiers: LCCN 2022016456 (print) | LCCN 2022016457 (ebook) | ISBN
  9781636080284 (paperback) | ISBN 9781636080291 (ebook)
Subjects: LCSH: Christian life. | Theology.
Classification: LCC BV4501.3 .J666 2022 (print) | LCC BV4501.3 (ebook) |
  DDC 248.4--dc23/eng/20220407
LC record available at https://lccn.loc.gov/2022016456
LC ebook record available at https://lccn.loc.gov/2022016457

Printed in the United States of America

Contents

Who Was Clarence Jordan?

Frederick L. Downing

IN 1942, at the height of World War II and more than a decade before the civil rights movement, a young pastor and farmer named Clarence Jordan founded Koinonia Farm, an interracial, pacifist communal experiment on depleted farmland in the Deep South, as a "demonstration plot for the kingdom of God." People needed to see the good news lived out in a practical life of justice where black and white Christians ate and worked together in harmony with one another and the earth.

BORN ON July 29, 1912, in Talbotton, Georgia, Clarence Leonard Jordan grew up in a conservative, privileged home. His father, Jim Jordan, had developed several businesses and owned farmland; he was mayor of Talbotton and head of its bank. Clarence's mother, Maude Jossey Jordan, had a great impact on his personal development. Her father had died in a gun accident, so she hated firearms and any form of fighting. People who knew her described her as particularly tenderhearted and sensitive. Like other white families in town, the couple raised their family in the Southern Baptist tradition.

On visits to the Jordans' landholdings, Clarence and his brothers would play with the fieldworkers' children. Clarence soon realized his playmates lived in dire poverty and had only a few months' schooling per year because their parents depended on their help with fieldwork. When they did attend school, they had to walk several miles to a one-room schoolhouse staffed by a teacher with minimal education. Clarence wondered why they couldn't come to the big school in Talbotton. He also wondered about a Sunday school song that said, "Jesus loves the little children, all the children of the world. Red and yellow, black and white, they are precious in his sight." If that was true, why were black children treated so differently?

Soon after his twelfth birthday, Clarence made his profession of faith during the yearly August revival. A family acquaintance, Mr. MacDonald, attended the same church and sang in the choir. He was also warden of the Talbot County Jail. The jail was a couple hundred yards behind the Jordans' home. At four o'clock every morning, a gong sounded to rouse the chain gang. The jail had five or six metal-barred wagons for transporting these prisoners to various worksites under the surveillance of armed guards.

A friend of Clarence's father's was imprisoned there – for killing a man over a love affair – and Clarence would join his father on visits. The boy became acquainted with others incarcerated there and often stopped to chat on his way home from school. Ed Russell was one who befriended him. Most of the inmates were black. In the course of conversation, they told him about the jail's "stretcher," in which a man being punished had his feet clamped to the floor while his arms were stretched upward with block and tackle.

Late one night, Clarence was wakened by terrible cries and groans from the direction of the jail – his friend Ed Russell's voice. The stretcher was in use, and Clarence could picture the man operating it – Mr. MacDonald, whose rich bass voice had proclaimed during Sunday evening service, "Love so mighty and so true merits my soul's best songs. / Faithful, loving service, too, to Him belongs. / Love lifted me . . ."

"That nearly tore me to pieces," Clarence would recall later. "I identified totally with that man in the stretcher. His agony was my agony." The appalling breach between what his religion professed and the brutality and violence he witnessed would churn in Clarence throughout his life.

During his teen years Clarence said little about this inner turmoil. With two mules, Jib and Jody, he plowed his father's fields. He learned to ride a motorbike and won a daredevil's reputation among his friends and brothers, with whom he explored the woods and creeks outside town. But his mind was active, too, and during high school he considered pursuing law in order to fight for justice for people like the men he knew in jail.

As head of the bank, Jim Jordan oversaw tenants on bank-owned land. Accompanying his father on his rounds brought Clarence face to face with the sharecropping system. The more he saw of rural Talbot County, the more he realized that "most of the blacks did not end up on the chain gang" – instead, they were held down by economic oppression. They needed justice in every area of life. So Clarence began to think that studying agriculture might better empower him to "help the poor lift the awful burden off their backs." He would share scientific knowledge with tenant farmers and help improve their lot.

In 1929, at seventeen, Clarence started classes in agriculture at the University of Georgia. But by the time he earned his degree, he no longer believed that better farming techniques alone could cure society's ills. He decided to pursue the ministry.

ALL MALE STUDENTS at the University of Georgia were expected to join the Reserve Officers Training Corps, and Clarence had signed on at the outset of his college career. After completing the compulsory two years, he volunteered for two additional years of advanced training. In June 1933 – after graduating from university and before starting seminary – he was set to receive his commission after a final ROTC camp in Gainesville, Georgia. This turned out to be a second turning point. Clarence was twenty-one.

He had been reading the Sermon on the Mount in Matthew's Gospel. One morning, when his officer commanded him to shoot at cardboard figures and impale straw dummies from horseback, he remembered Jesus' words, "Love your enemies." Cantering through the designated woodland, Clarence suddenly saw these targets as

the enemies Jesus had told his followers to love. In that
moment, he grasped that Jesus and the US Army taught
opposite values. He reined in his horse and dismounted.
Walking out of the woods, he handed his pistol, spurs,
and saber to the officer in charge.

From the moment that he got down off of his horse
in Gainesville to turn in his weapons, Clarence Jordan
began a journey toward radical discipleship – living
out the commands of Jesus unconditionally. Clarence
trained for the ministry at Southern Baptist Theological
Seminary in Louisville, Kentucky. Here he learned to
read the Bible in Greek and Hebrew. More importantly,
he came to see that "the Word must come alive in currents of history and social change." Learning to read
the Bible in this way led him to see that the earliest
Christian church was a *koinonia,* a communal fellowship
of economic sharing. In time, he became convinced that
Christians needed a new theory of economics – one of
sharing based on need.

When Clarence joined other seminarians at a
mission in Louisville's ghetto, he was surprised to learn
how many of the inner-city destitute were from rural
Alabama and Georgia. This experience "drove me to
get back to the area that was vomiting these people up,

to see if we couldn't reverse the trend from the farms to the city." He felt that if the problems of race and poverty were to be solved, it must be "in the regions where tensions are the greatest, and rooted in the poor economy of the South."

In seminary, Clarence met Florence Kroeger, a young woman who worked in the library. More than her blue eyes, her sense of adventure and willingness to take risks drew him to her. As their friendship grew, he confided in her his dream of returning to the Deep South to help the poor. And when their relationship became serious, he told her, "If you want to be the wife of a pastor of the First Baptist church someplace, you don't want to marry me." Florence was undeterred, and they were married on July 21, 1936.

WHILE IN LOUISVILLE, Clarence Jordan came to see the American church as under the powerful sway of a plantation mentality, with controlling cultural myths about race, nation, and wealth that created a rift between the life of the spirit and the daily life of the believer. Clarence developed a two-pronged strategy to counteract this bifurcation of life. First, he would make a Bible version with the stories set in the American South

and told in the language of the cotton patch so common
people could see the Bible as good news for the poor
and become participants instead of spectators. Second,
society needed a demonstration plot – a concrete example
and daily reminder of an authentic Christian life.

So, at age thirty, in 1942, Clarence moved onto a
440-acre farm he had located near Americus, in south-
west Georgia. He named it Koinonia. Another couple,
Martin and Mabel England, joined the Jordans' venture.
Clarence and Florence had two children, Eleanor and
James, by this time; the Englands had children as well.
Koinonia became the lived example Clarence had envi-
sioned, interracial and communal. "It scared the devil
out of us to think of going against Southern traditions,"
Clarence later confessed.

It would also take a lot of work. The red clay soil was
badly eroded, and the buildings so rundown that the
two men moved in first to make the homes habitable
for their families. Clarence chose a one-room shack in a
lonesome spot for his office. Here he could read, think,
pray, and start drafting his Cotton Patch Version of the
New Testament.

The two families joined the local church, Rehoboth
Baptist. So did other Koinonia members, as the

community grew. For a time, there was relative calm surrounding Koinonia's endeavors. Clarence sought to be a good neighbor and to go slow with his revolutionary ideas. But Koinonia Farm was established in the middle of World War II, and Clarence's antiwar sentiments offended his neighbors. In 1949, accusations reached the FBI that he "counseled young men against entering military service." Had this charge been proven, he would have been guilty of sedition, in violation of the Selective Service Act of 1948. The FBI gathered evidence and interviewed Clarence, but the US Attorney in Macon declined to prosecute him.

Another time, a group of men arrived at the farm, asking for Clarence Jordan and identifying themselves as Ku Klux Klan. When Clarence introduced himself, one of them glared into his face. "We're here to tell you that we don't allow the sun to set on anybody who eats with n-----s." Without missing a beat, Clarence grabbed the man's right hand and began pumping. "I'm a Baptist preacher and I just graduated from the Southern Baptist seminary," he grinned. "I've heard about people who had power over the sun, but I never hoped to meet one."

In August 1950, the Rehoboth Baptist Church voted to expel Clarence and the other Koinonians from the church because they had "brought people of other races into the services." After this event, Clarence would never join another denomination or local church. Instead, he viewed himself as a member of the church universal and expanded his conversation with churches outside the Southern Baptist orbit. He also depended more on the brothers and sisters of the community for spiritual fellowship. "Something has been set in motion here, something that is eternal," Clarence declared. "I'm beginning to see that I'm in this thing called Koinonia for life."

Half a week after the eviction, elderly Baptist deacon Bowen arrived at Koinonia to ask forgiveness. "Well, you have it," Clarence replied. Bowen asked if they could pray, and the two knelt on the bare clay beneath a tree in the yard.

As the old man stood to go he said, "I can't go into a church that won't have you in it."

"You don't get out of the church," Clarence countered. "You live so that they kick you out."

THE DECADE of the 1950s would be increasingly violent for Clarence Jordan and Koinonia. The Supreme Court's 1954 ruling in *Brown v. Board of Education,* with its mandate to desegregate public schools, was a watershed event in American culture and a direct challenge to the status quo in American race relations. In 1956, two young black men contacted Clarence Jordan. They wanted to enroll at the Georgia State College of Business, but every applicant had to produce signatures from two alumni of Georgia's university system – a gambit that had always prevented any black student from entering. Clarence drove to Atlanta to meet the prospective students and offer his support.

By the time he got back to his community three hours later, the state governor had called the Sumter County sheriff with instructions to "check out this Jordan fellow." That night, the anonymous threatening phone calls began. Some nights they came every ten minutes, from sunset till morning.

In the months that followed there were twenty-eight separate attacks against Koinonia, including the use of dynamite, firebombs, and high-powered rifles. Koinonia had grown to about sixty people, black and white, and they were all in danger. One night, when Eleanor Jordan, home from college, turned on her bedroom light, a bullet ripped through her bedroom wall, missing her by inches. Luckily, the attacks killed no one.

Senator Joe McCarthy had whipped up anti-communist sentiment, adding grist to the rumor mill of Americus, Georgia. Clarence Jordan must be communist, locals reckoned, for he had refused to support the war effort, his race-mixing was well known, and out-of-state cars had been observed at Koinonia. A local grand jury investigated Jordan and Koinonia. Its report, which it sent to the Department of Justice, concluded that Koinonia profited from the violence, that Clarence Jordan committed perjury, and that he was lacking in "honesty, integrity, and good faith." Koinonia was accused of spreading false propaganda and keeping blacks in "a state of brainwashed peonage."

In 1957 the Ku Klux Klan again trained its sights on Koinonia. On Sunday, February 27, they gathered from across the state at the Americus fairgrounds, 150 strong, in robes and hoods. Their rally began with a prayer and ended with a motorcade that drove slowly past the farm. One of the Koinonia children said, years later, that this was the first time he saw fear in the faces of community adults.

BY THE END of the 1950s, many people had left Koinonia – some driven away by fear, others just ready to move on. The community was a shadow of its former self, and Clarence Jordan had to find new ways of envisioning his mission. As he read the Bible in economic terms, he sought a way to redistribute land and wealth to the poor and dispossessed. He created Koinonia Partners, a revision of his original idea of Koinonia, to build houses for the poor at cost and at no interest (it was the forerunner of Habitat for Humanity). And he established a Fund for Humanity to restore land to the poor.

He also began speaking widely at churches and colleges. His early writings had struck an optimistic tone. Now his sermons, like those given at Goshen College in 1965, tended to focus on the hard teachings of Jesus, such as renouncing wealth and learning to love one's enemies. In his writing and preaching, he grew more daring in calling for change in the church and in the lives of Christians. He now addressed Christian institutions and individuals bluntly: "You ought to spend at least as much trying to help house your poor brothers whom you have seen as trying to house God whom you have never seen." He was angered when a Georgia church spent twenty-five thousand dollars installing a decorative fountain while there were people in town with no running water. And when a minister bragged that his congregation had just erected a ten-thousand-dollar cross, Clarence retorted, "Time was when Christians could get those for free."

After the death of Martin Luther King Jr. in 1968, Clarence Jordan became even more resolute. In a sermon titled "Things Needed for Our Peace," given less than a month after King's assassination, Clarence boldly condemned American racism in a way that remains contemporary more than fifty years later. He called on the privileged students of Furman University to go out from that place with a new spirit of servanthood. And at the American Baptist Convention meeting in Seattle in the summer of 1969, he urged pastors to focus their ministry in the here and now rather than pointing believers away from this world.

Clarence would still disappear into his shack in the pecan orchard to reflect, pray, and write. His belief that Jesus invited his followers to a revolutionary way of life – its marching orders contained in the Sermon on the Mount – never wavered. During the 1960s, he labored over his Cotton Patch version of the Gospels.

After King's death, with racial tensions still strong, the FBI continued to follow Clarence Jordan closely. On August 24, 1969, he accompanied two black Christians to the First Methodist Church of Americus. They were refused entry. Clarence and the other two remained outside and attempted to talk to worshippers when they came out. A report on this event was sent to the FBI and other intelligence units.

Two months later, on October 29, 1969, Clarence was working on his Cotton Patch Version of the Gospel of John in his writing shack when he suffered a massive heart attack and died. He was fifty-seven.

Clarence Jordan's prophetic voice was a corrective to an overly spiritualized Christianity, bringing into sharp focus the radical nature of the Christian gospel as it relates to materialism, militarism, and racism. He was a hero to some and a thorn to many. He delivered his Master's message in the vernacular of his own people and place, but, more importantly, he showed all of us that it can and must come to expression in our daily lives.

Frederick L. Downing, professor of philosophy and religious studies at Valdosta State University, also selected the readings in this volume. He is the author of *Clarence Jordan: A Radical Pilgrimage in Scorn of the Consequences*; *Elie Wiesel: A Religious Biography*; and *To See the Promised Land: The Faith Pilgrimage of Martin Luther King, Jr.*

Reading Clarence Jordan Today

Starlette Thomas

BEFORE YOU TURN THE PAGE and enter the life of Clarence Jordan through his own words, it's worth taking stock of where Christianity in North America finds itself these days, more than half a century after his death.

You might be as puzzled as I am. Didn't Jesus call himself "the way"? How hard could it be for his disciples to keep their eyes on him, to keep walking straight in the way he showed us? Turns out his way is also pretty narrow, and few find it (Matt. 7:14).

Hyperpoliticized and evenly divided on who's wrong and who's right, the North American church continues to toe "the color line." Not much has changed in five decades: we're still segregated at 11 a.m. on Sunday. The sociopolitical construct of race still holds the reins, controlling the ways in which Christian communities of faith are formed in most places. We still avoid talking about race, but we'll sing in a well-meaning way: "Jesus loves the little children, all the children of the world. Red and yellow, black and white, they are precious in his sight."

But that's not how Jesus loves the little children. It is well past time that we deracialize his gospel, as his love is not color-coded. God's love is unconditional, which means it is uncategorical.

Besides, we're not supposed to see our bodies that way. Paul wrote to the believers at Corinth: "Even though we once knew Jesus from a human point of view, we know him no longer in that way. So, if anyone is in Christ, there is a new creation: everything old has passed away; see, everything has become new!" (2 Cor. 5:16–17). Or as Clarence Jordan put it in The Second Letter to the Atlanta Christians: "That's why, from here on out, we pay absolutely no attention to a person's outward appearance. It is true that we once knew Christ physically, but now we do so no longer. Therefore, if a man is a Christian he is a brand-new creation. The old guy is gone: look, a new man has appeared."

To be clear, this call for a raceless gospel is not a suggestion that we be colorblind, and it is not a vision of what some have described as a post-racial society. Instead, it is an invitation to see race as it really is: a caste system with a good paint job. This raceless gospel is also a proclamation of an undivided "kin-dom" to come. Until then, we should see race as the good news of socially colored white skin and therefore "another gospel" (Gal. 6–9). In *Cotton Patch Parables for Liberation,* Clarence Jordan writes, "The church of God does not respect color lines." But Jordan didn't just write it down; he lived it out, "precept upon precept, line upon line" (Isa. 28:13).

Clarence and Florence Jordan, with Martin and Mabel England and a few others, drew a line in the sand at Koinonia Farm in Americus, Georgia, in 1942. Right then, not waiting for a more appropriate time, they bore witness to the hospitality, kinship, and fellowship of Christ's body. Jordan said, "Faith is not belief in spite of the evidence, but a life in scorn of the consequences." Academically trained and ordained, he knew what he was talking about. But his farmer's hands called him to do some deep digging in American soil foreign to this kind of Christian witnessing. As he worked the land, he toiled with the issues of race and its progeny as a spiritual discipline. It was important for Jordan that he lived it, that he brought it home, even though it was inconvenient.

Jordan called Koinonia Farm his "demonstration plot," where he dared to erase "the color line" by integrating his faith and his life, practicing it in community with African Americans, those socially colored black. It was forbidden, this so-called race-mixing, and he no doubt crossed the line. He got the Ku Klux Klan's attention and the group paid him several visits, leaving bullets as they drove by. But Jordan kept his head down, and his head was on straight; he was a pacifist who founded a desegregated community because he was grounded in his faith. He saw that the American church was following in the footsteps of the American empire, and he went another way.

Perhaps Jordan had a vision like that of Peter, who reported back to the New Members Committee of the church at Jerusalem: "The Spirit told me to go with them and not to make a distinction between them and us" (Acts 11:12). Despite the disapproval of his neighbors, who cut ties and boycotted the farm, Jordan kept on digging and planting seeds in hopes that the church would change. He showed that you don't need much to make a difference.

We are all God's children. What a shame it is that much of the North American church has chosen an Enlightenment idea about identity over the truth that we are all created in the image of God. Coloring in the face of God in peach tones, we have framed the divine in 11 x 17 and hung up an idolized version of ourselves in our homes and sanctuaries.

Careful not to change a thing, it seems that the North American church is, by and large, stuck in a time past, or perhaps walking back on its calling to be the reconciling body of Christ. Christianity is not following its leader. This is not a new insight but a necessary confession. From Jesus' first handpicked disciples until now, Christian believers have been a walking contradiction, with Jesus saying one thing and his followers doing another. These discrepancies have caused many Christians and onlookers to question whether the church is the right body for the job. Because it needs bodywork.

I found Clarence Jordan's words when I was looking at Christianity, realizing that in remaining segregated on Sunday mornings it wasn't just missing something but missing the point. In Jordan, I stumbled upon a guide who knew exactly where I expected my faith to take me, who shared my convictions, and whose faith had led him to defy the status quo. A Greek-reading green thumb, Clarence Jordan stuck out to me. I couldn't unsee the cotton patch evidence.

Jordan didn't wait on the world to change. Instead, he changed the world around him. He didn't wait on the laws to change; instead, he followed the laws of Christ. He lived in his own world, which proved to me that there is life outside of and apart from this racialized reality. It could be done, and I didn't have to wait on the North American church to do it. No, I could put my hands to the plow and turn my corner of the world upside down.

YOU MAY BE WONDERING how my connection to Clarence Jordan came about, how a twenty-first-century African American pastor finds herself enthusing about a Jim Crow–era Southern Baptist minister. You could say we were brought together by the Holy Spirit and a shared commitment to building community. A few years ago, I received a pastoral study grant from the Louisville Institute in Kentucky, supported by the Lilly Endowment, to take a sabbatical and undertake a deep dive into Clarence Jordan's life and writings.

At the time, I was questioning my faith in race and in the North American expression of Christianity, which supports it, evidenced by the fact that its churches come in black and white. Today, I have no doubt that American Christianity is complicit in oppression due to its silent, even unwitting, trading in the perks and privileges of white supremacy. I am not alone; there have always been Christians who sensed that the church was not living up to its confessions, that it had somehow lost its way, that it would need witnesses who could shine a light when the church hid its own light for power, position, or material gain.

Christians in America must answer for the many ways that they do not identify with the way of Jesus or answer his call for justice. Far too many are wishy-washy, fifty-fifty, feigning laryngitis and pretending they cannot find their voice to answer the blood calling from the ground. Still, I must ask: Were you there for sweet Elijah McClain, who went to the store for snacks but never made it back home? Were you there for Ahmaud Arbery, stopped in his tracks while jogging? Were you there when they shot Breonna Taylor while she lay in bed sleeping? Were you there when they choked the life out of George Floyd? When bowed heads at Mother Emanuel AME Church were filled with bullets? When supermarket shoppers in Buffalo, New York, were murdered in the aisles? Because if we aren't there for them, then why are we here? If these deaths don't affect you personally, how can we talk about being one nation, let alone the one body of Christ?

Word made flesh, Jesus is God on the ground, on the move, where the injustice is. Jesus is in the thick of it. Jesus is God face to face, in places we think he wouldn't be caught dead and with the last people we would picture him with. As his disciples, we should be close on his heels and always be found in his company – no matter who he is keeping company with.

Unfortunately, instead of being known for "sharing all things in common" as the first Christians were, American Christians are known for shoving select scriptures down people's throats. Nauseated by this and no longer wanting to be associated with the likes of such Christians, many followers of Jesus have left the church building and are looking for him elsewhere. They know that he is found in community: at shared tables, at sickbeds, and at gravesides; with tortured souls; with those who secretly are interested yet don't want to be seen with him; with women and children.

For years, I had searched for a conversation partner who could double as a witness to this gnawing, nagging yearning for authentic being and belonging in Christian community – without the surveillance of race. I wanted to be seen fully, freely, and authentically, apart from "the white gaze." I needed to prove that it could be done, not just personally but in community. For me, that witness was Clarence Jordan. He made me believe again that there could be more to human being and belonging.

So, as part of my project, which looked at the malformation of Christian community due to the sociopolitical construct of race, I studied Clarence Jordan's writings and his witness at Koinonia Farm. I wanted to know more about the man who broke the laws of segregation to keep the law of love, which Jesus distilled for us in the Greatest Commandment, to "love your neighbor as yourself" (Matt. 22:35–40).

On Koinonia Farm's seventy-fifth anniversary, I walked the grounds and stood just outside Clarence Jordan's writing shack. I pictured him writing there. I wanted to be close to him, close to someone who kept their convictions even closer. My feet were dug in by then. I looked around and took in his handiwork, pecans on the ground ready to be harvested. His Christian identity was not a card he carried but a role he carried out and acted out in the world, and quite literally planted in the ground.

These observations led me to believe that the churches in North America will either be communal or coffins. There is no life in spaces cut off from entire communities. Churches will either be inclusive or invisible to generations who have no interest in hand-me-down hatreds, exclusionary prejudices, and sacred stereotypes. Going to these churches will make no difference if they offer the same selections and preferences as American society at large.

There is a generation that wants to see something different. And we are willing to go to the ends of the earth, and back in time, to find those who know the way – a way out of racialized identities and hierarchical forms of belonging in a capitalist society. For me and for many others, Clarence Jordan is one of those. A patron saint of community-builders, he still speaks to those who feel called to defy race and its categorized way of living. He inspires us to lay to rest this segregated expression of church and demonstrate a better way.

Starlette Thomas, a Baptist minister, is director of The Raceless Gospel Initiative at Good Faith Ministries and host of the Raceless Gospel *podcast.*

I

Impractical Christianity

The following article appeared in Young People's Quarterly *in 1948, "written from personal experience as director of Koinonia Farm, a Christian agricultural missionary project in Georgia."*

YOU CAN'T PUT Christianity into practice. You can't *make* it work. As desperately as it is needed in this poor, broken world, it is *not* a philosophy of life to be "tried." Nor is it a social or ethical ideal which has tantalized humankind with the possibility of attainment.

For Christianity is not a system you work – it is a Person who works you. You don't get *it*; he gets *you*. Jesus said, "I am . . . the life" (John 14:6). Now life isn't something you try out for a while and then exchange for something else if it doesn't prove practical. You either have it or you don't. And if your Christianity is the kind that has to be "worked," you don't have the real thing. For when you look long and deeply into the face of

Jesus, that compulsion of love falls on you, and you find yourself vowing that you would follow him and serve him – practical or impractical, wise or foolish, for better or worse – unto the death.

Somehow or other we simply must realize this. Already too many people are thinking of Christianity as a glorified scheme which will gather up all the frayed ends of our social, industrial, economic, and political reforms into a golden fabric of peace and plenty. "Everything else has failed," people say, "let's try Christianity" – as though it were a jigsaw puzzle awaiting human ingenuity to put it together! We talk of reconstruction; Jesus talks about rebirth. The city of God is not built up from below; it comes down from the Father.

Christianity is more than a scheme to be tried – it is a guiding star. Christians are those who locate and direct themselves by Christ, just as a navigator takes bearings from a fixed star. What Jesus taught and accomplished among us has given us our knowledge of God. His word and way are more dependable than the North Star, and whenever we navigate by him, we can be sure of arriving. By getting our sight on Jesus, we get our bearings; we are no longer "lost," for we know where we are and where we are going. And it isn't the star that is practical or impractical, but the navigator who accepts or rejects its guiding light.

But at the time Jesus spoke these words, I suppose the world considered those who followed him as foolish, impractical, idealistic, fanatic. He made them forsake jobs and homes; he led them across racial boundaries when the time was anything but ripe; he turned them into peacemakers when the popular thing to do was to hate. And in return, he rewarded them with a cross!

Would any but fools follow such a one? Yet they couldn't help it. Never once did they ask: "Aren't we going a bit too fast? Won't we do more harm than good by stirring up the people?" Perhaps as Jesus set his face toward Jerusalem and certain death, Thomas spoke for them all when he said, "Let us also go, that we may die with him" (John 11:16). The statement of a fool – a fool for Christ!

Such compulsion is not the product of reason but of love. And love has its roots in fellowship. They were with him, they followed him, they knew him, they loved him. This fellowship with him changed them, empowered them. And herein is the clue to our weakness and the key to our possibilities.

For what we need more than goods is God; more than a living is life. Even though we build with our own hands a new world, if we find not God, our lives still are voids darkened by the lurking shadows of our own selfishness and echoing to the whimperings of children who won't admit they are lost.

Have you ever imagined what you would do if you could be alone with Christ for a few hours? You think you would ask him all kinds of questions and discuss with him the many perplexing problems which plague our fear-haunted world. But you wouldn't. For a while you would just sit and look at him. Then, as though drawn by a magnet, you would come near him and kneel. And while you knelt, he would put his hands upon you in loving forgiveness, and you would feel indescribable peace and power surging through you. You would lift up your eyes and look into his. But you wouldn't, you couldn't, ask him anything.

You would be in that silent, wordless fellowship which love alone interprets. Fellowship with him is all the heaven one seeks, the answer to all problems, the goal of all yearnings, the fulfilment of all desire.

2

The Meaning of Christian Fellowship

This article appeared in the Spring 1946 issue of Prophetic Religion: A Journal of Christian Faith and Action, *published by the Fellowship of Southern Churchmen.*

FROM POPULOUS CITY and desolate wilderness has gone up the universal cry of lonely hearts for fellowship. We have sought for it in amusement places; we have pursued it through the halls of learning. We have organized it into clubs, lodges, fraternities, and "fellowships." We have given it thousands of banquets – interracial, international, intereverything. Committees, leagues, and councils have spaded the social order in quest of it. And at times we have gone wistfully and hopefully to church, feeling that we would catch a glimpse there of this elusive pearl of great price.

Perhaps we haven't really known what we were searching for. And in our desperate hunger, we have been willing to accept any cheap substitute which offered a measure of relief. These substitutes have been delightful to the taste, but give no nourishment.

As a matter of fact, nowhere in the New Testament does the word "fellowship" appear in the sense of pleasant social contacts. It is a translation of the Greek word *koinonia,* which Thayer's Lexicon defines as "fellowship, association, community, communion, joint participation." Of these definitions, the most accurate is "community," or better, "a commune." The adjective, *koine,* means "common" and the verb, *koinoneo,* means "to hold in common."

The word occurs several times in the New Testament, one of which is in Acts 2:42: "And they continued steadfastly in the apostles' doctrine and in the *koinonia* (commune), and in breaking of bread, and in prayers." What koinonia? The one which Luke is about to describe when he continues: "And all that believed were together, and had all things common (*koine*), and sold their possessions and goods and distributed them to everybody, according as any one had need" (Acts 2:44–45). Careful historian that he was, Luke never used repetition except for decided emphasis. Evidently he attached unusual importance to the *koinonia,* for he again describes it in Acts 4:32–5:11. "Now the heart and mind of the crowd of believers was one, and nobody said any of his possessions to be his own, but all things were common to them."

Such a radical departure from the slave-economy pattern could be attributed to but one thing: the Lord Jesus had been raised and was alive in their midst. Other people looked with surprise but also with favor upon people whose lives were so transformed that "there wasn't a needy person among them, for whoever had fields or houses sold them and brought the proceeds and turned them in to the apostles. And it was distributed to each according to his need" (Acts 4:34–35).

This description of the *koinonia,* or fellowship, or commune, is followed by two examples of how it was received. Barnabas complied fully, for he brought all the proceeds from his sale. But Ananias and Sapphira, desiring the fellowship but unwilling to pay the price, brought "a certain part," which was probably the tithe required by Jewish law (Acts 5:2). Peter's severity with them was not due to the desperate need of the disciples for funds but to Ananias's and Sapphira's flagrant violation of the spirit of the *koinonia.* Had they been allowed to come on into the fellowship without passing the acid test, no doubt they would have been first to instigate opposition to the group's broad views on race. For the mistletoe of prejudice thrives nowhere better than on the economic oak.

Now where did the disciples get the idea of such a fellowship? Was it a sudden outcropping of the intense spiritual experience of Pentecost? Or was it the natural expression of something they had been familiar with and had had training in?

Only the latter could possibly have been the case. It was so completely different from prevailing customs that without an *authoritative precedent* they could never have been "of one heart and mind," even at Pentecost (Acts 4:32). And it seems highly improbable that such a profound plan affecting the entire life of everyone could have been the product of little or no thought. Full approval and participation by the apostles, who claimed now as never before to be led by the resurrected Lord, can be explained only by the fact that the originator of the plan was Jesus.

For three years they had been taught by Jesus to love one another. Upon love – of God and man – hung the law and the prophets. It was to be the distinguishing mark of the Christian. "By this shall people know that you are my disciples, that you love one another" (John 13:35). But Jesus was no philosopher, and he never conceived of *abstract love.* To him love was definite, positive. Perhaps John was quoting him when he wrote: "Let us put our love not into words or into talk but into deeds, and make it real" (1 John 3:18).

It was quite natural, then, that for him love should signify a definite relationship. It must lead to "marriage," so to speak. . . . In other words, when do we set up the relationship to which real love inevitably leads?

So when Jesus called his disciples, he was establishing, in effect, a *family* upon spiritual rather than blood ties. "Who is my brother and my sister? . . . He that doeth the will of him who sent me" (Mark 3:33–35). And we find that the little *koinonia* of twelve which he established and which was the nucleus of the Pentecost fellowship embodied the same fundamental principles as the family, the most persistent of human institutions.

The first requirement for discipleship was *common ownership* – to "forsake all." This does not mean that Peter, James, and John abandoned their nets and left them to rot on the seashore. These same nets were probably used frequently to replenish the common treasury, and were in good shape on the night after the crucifixion when Peter and others decided to go fishing. But these nets were not Peter's. He had forsaken them. They now belonged to the group.

Before the rich young ruler was invited to follow Jesus, he was commanded to get rid of all his private property. When Zacchaeus committed himself to voluntary poverty, Jesus said, "This day has salvation come to this house" (Luke 19:9). The poor widow was commended because she cast in "*all*" her living" (Luke 21:1–4). Matthew gave up a lucrative job and all that went with it. In fact, could we imagine the disciples attaining their high degree of fellowship without absolute economic equality?

Now this need not be an occasion of stumbling for us. Upon every hand there is abundant illustration that this is a natural expression of intense love. A man will gladly or willingly vow: "With all my goods I thee endow." When my three-year-old son crawls up in my lap and says, "Put down your book, daddy," I must confess I am no longer a rugged individualist, mumbling something about private property. I say with the Loving Father of the elder brother, "Son . . . all that I have is thine" (Luke 15:31). A man will say the same thing to a brother whom he truly loves. And if love will cause a man to lay down his life for a friend, will it not lead him to cheerfully lay down his goods?

It is evident that this is by no means the philosophy of Russian communism. While communism is the result in both cases, the motivation is vastly different. One is the voluntary product of love, the other the involuntary product of force.

But are people capable of such complete, voluntary fellowship? The illustrations given above prove that they are not only capable but actually practice it. . . . Among the Kachin tribes of Burma there are no capitalists. All land is owned by the tribe. It is pathetic how we Christians faint before attaining even pagan heights. And in our stupor we pat ourselves on the back for our fine spirit of fellowship when we attend a meeting where a person of another race might be present!

The second principle of the *koinonia,* or spiritual family, was *distribution according to need.* There was nothing particularly new about this, for it was described as the method of distributing manna in the wilderness. "This is the thing which the Lord hath commanded, gather of it every man according to his eating, an omer for every man, according to the number of your persons; take ye every man for them which are in his tents" (Exod.

16:16). It was then measured out to every man according to his dependents regardless of how much he had gathered, or how educated he was, or how responsible his position, or how great his influence, or how insatiable his greed. On this basis, "he that gathered much had nothing over, and he that gathered little had no lack." There were some hoarders then as now, but by the next morning the manna was spoiled. Here was an airtight ration system.

Surely Jesus was thoroughly familiar with this system, and no doubt practiced it with the twelve. That is why it became a very natural part of the larger *koinonia* after Pentecost. It so happened, however, that this was the occasion for the first quarrel among the early Christians. All had agreed that distribution should be made on the basis of need, but soon it was being made according to culture. The Grecians were given less than the Hebrews, who no doubt were the administrators. When this was called to the attention of the apostles, there was immediately set up a board of deacons, all of whom had Greek names, to see that distribution was impartially done. The original function of a deacon, then, was not to call a preacher nor to dictate his message, but simply to serve as a member of a scrupulously honest ration board.

That the principle is a sound one is proved by the fact that practically the whole civilized world adopted it during the war emergency, and while there was much complaining, no thinking person condemned the system as basically unfair. The flaws were in people and methods, not in the principle.

So then, the pressure of circumstances forced the pagan world to a measure that love should have been constraining Christians to practice all along.

The third principle of the Christian fellowship was *complete equality* and *freedom of every believer, regardless of racial background.* Here again they got the idea from Jesus. When John wrote, "He must needs go through Samaria" (John 4:4), it was not a geographical but a moral necessity. Jesus couldn't Jim Crow the Samaritans. To a proud, aristocratic, blue-blooded Jewish lawyer, he told the story of the Good Samaritan, with more emphasis on *Samaritan* than on *good.* When publicans and sinners were drawing near to him and he was rebuked by the Pharisees for keeping such company, he told the story of the Loving Father and his two sons.

Twice, with fiery zeal, he cleansed the Temple. Was such anger kindled because of a bazaar in the basement? He explains his wrath by quoting Isaiah: ". . . my house shall be called a house of prayer for *all* people" (Isa. 56:7). We may be certain that the Court of the Jews was in good shape, as was the Holy of Holies, but into the Court of the Gentiles, where *people* at prayer should have been, prejudice and greed had brought *animals.* By his act, Jesus restored the evacuated Gentiles to their lawful place in the "house of prayer for *all* people."

From these, as well as many other experiences, the disciples learned the full significance of the command to "preach the gospel to *every* creature" (Mark 16:15). And the whole Book of Acts is simply the unfolding story of Christianity overflowing racial boundaries – from Jew to Samaritan to Gentile. It could well be the Christian's handbook on race relations.

Such, then, was the meaning of Christian fellowship for the early disciples. Whether or not we can have it depends largely upon our willingness to pay the price.

Perhaps the time is ripe for some rather bold experimentation along this line. Of course, it would call for a measure of devotion and courage far beyond that which Christians generally are accustomed to and, in many respects, it would be equivalent to a new birth. But here are the seeds of a world revolution, which must come sooner or later. When and how it comes depends upon

Christians, who have the keys of the kingdom. If they fail to use the keys, humanity will batter down the door, for it knows that it must get in or die.

3

What Is the Word of God?

*The following is taken from a talk Clarence Jordan
gave at a Baptist church in Brookings, South Dakota,
on December 3, 1952.*

IT IS OF EXTREME IMPORTANCE that we have a
clear understanding of the relationship between the
church and the Word of God which gives it guidance
and direction. What is the Word of God? Well, what's
the meaning of "word"? The dictionary says: "A vehicle
for the conveyance of an idea." I have something in
mind, and I want to get it over to you and put it in your
mind. I use words with which to do it; they convey the
thought, the idea, from my mind to your mind. Now in a
sense, the Word of God is that transmission of God's will
and purposes to his people. It is the communication of
himself to those who allow themselves to be part of the
extension of the incarnation.

Now when we come to discuss just what this Word is, we find that the supreme act of God's revelation, the communication of himself to us, is the gift of his Son, Jesus Christ. Jesus is the Word of God. We read in the Bible that the Word became flesh. It does not say the Word became ink. Not a book – the Word became a man and dwelt among us. And John said, "What we have heard, what we have seen, what we have handled, of the Word of truth, that declare we unto you" (1 John 1:1–2). They spoke to an experience about a person, Jesus Christ. So the Word of God is his Son made flesh.

The Word of God, then, was in the beginning. It was before the King James Version – that might surprise you, but it was. Some people seem to think that Jesus just happened to have gotten hold of a King James Version Bible and came to earth trying to fit himself into it. I'm sorry – the King James Version just wasn't in the beginning. But it says the Word was, and it became flesh in Jesus Christ; it did not become a book. He preceded the written word; he did not follow it.

So, then, the New Testament is not a blueprint but an account of those things which have happened among us, as Luke says. It did not set the thing up and then try to fit God's plans and purposes into it. Many of us as we approach the Bible try to fit Jesus into it as one would try to fit oneself into a suit of clothes, instead of trying to fit the suit of clothes to oneself. He did not come to fit into anyone's concept of a messianic expectation. The written word is of any value only as it testifies of him. He is Lord not only of the Sabbath but also of the Bible, the written word. By him all preaching, past and present, and all writing, past and present, must be judged. So, then, he was God's word to humankind; he is above the written page, above the book. He is God's communication, so that anyone who has seen the Son has seen the Father.

But how about us who didn't see him in the flesh? How are we to know? How does God communicate the Son to us, to every generation? The earlier writers said, "We saw him with our eyes, we heard him, we were eyewitnesses to those things that happened among us." And for a long time we knew only what those who saw him told of him. But then they passed away, and then came the job of making anew that communication to every generation.

The next way God communicates himself and makes known himself – his word to man – is by the written word, the Bible. As I said before, the written word is not *the* Word of God, it is but a witness to that Word. I come from a section of the country where folks say, "I believe that book from cover to cover, from Generations to Revolutions; every word in it is inspired of God – he just sat down one day at his dictaphone and rattled it off word for word. And Peter and James and John and Paul and the rest of them just took it down as they heard it from God." And they use it, and for some of them it takes the place of the Word of God. I wonder if some of my brethren down there don't break the Second Commandment by worshiping the Bible instead of God. Then I find too – up in some northern parts of the world too – that some folks don't know enough about it to worship it! At least some of those folks down there are concerned enough to say they believe it – some other folks that I know of aren't even concerned enough to read it.

But what about this book? What place does it have in the church? I would like to say that we must not use it as a prison for the living Word: we must not feel that it's a closed book, that it's a mold into which we are going to pour the church, into which we are going to pour everything. I read anyway where it says that Jesus said, "There are many things that I would like to say to you, but you cannot take them now" (John 16:12). Where are those many things, and when are they going to be made known to us? Doesn't he imply there is still a mystery, still some revelation that he will make to those of us who are his disciples yet to come? And John said, "There are many things that Jesus did that are not written in this book" (John 21:25).

If we are going to understand the Bible, three things are necessary:

1. We must be in the fellowship. Our hearts must be expectant, friendly, open to the Word. We must *want* to know, open to receive it when it comes. Jesus says anyone who does God's will "shall know of the doctrine, whether it be of God" (John 7:17). Now a person who studies it objectively as a book of history, or as any other book, never gets it. It's those who get inside the fellowship, and who love it and expect something from it, who understand it. If you're going to use the Bible at all, you're going to have to be its friend, not going there to find fault with it. How many times I have seen students going to it to find its errors. You can find them, but it will never speak to you. It will be as dumb as it can be; you'll never hear the still small voice that stirs your heart. It's only

those who go to it yearning, hungering, open, receptive, and friendly. Then the old book comes out of the pages, its words glow as if they were lit with neon, and the truth comes out to you. At times it makes your heart wonder if you can hold it all. When you really want to know – when the truth of God really comes flooding in on you – it's a great experience. If you have never had it, you ought to seek it.

2. If you are going to understand the Bible, the Holy Spirit must be your guide. Not the theological professor, not the preacher. Jesus says, "When he, the Spirit of truth, is come, he will guide you into all truth" (John 16:13). It is a book that can only be interpreted rightly by the Holy Spirit. And every time I read it, if it is going to mean anything to me, I must read it with the consciousness that it is the Spirit who is the teacher, and it is he who takes these written words and brings them out and lays them upon my mind, upon my heart – makes them come alive. The Spirit of truth makes the Bible living truth to me.

3. In the last place, you must make a response of obedience through faith. Why do you want to know? Why

should God make it known what is the truth? Have any of you ever gone to the cookbook to read recipes just for the joy of reading them? Pretty dry reading, isn't it? You go there and try to get knowledge and translate it into pies and cakes and gravy and biscuits and soufflés and all. I've been going around here eating among you folks, and you've been translating some of those recipes into mighty good stuff! Supposing I went to your house and you said, "Why, do you know, I just read the most wonderful recipe, oh, it's wonderful – won't you have some?" Well, it might be nice, but you want it for a purpose, that you might act upon it. I do not think God would make known his truth to people who have no intention of living it. Jesus said, "People don't light a lamp to put it under a basket, but they put it on a lampstand that it might shine to all those in the house" (Matt. 5:15). He says if people are not foolish enough to light up their lamps and put them under a basket, God is not foolish enough to light up his lamps and put them under a basket. If you want to be lighted up by the truth of God, remember that he lights it with a purpose: to shine to all who are in the house. You need not expect to get any more light until you live by that which you have already gotten.

Now, some of us want to delve into what was the meaning of Nebuchadnezzar's dream, or the meaning of Belshazzar's dream, or the meaning of the pale horse in Revelation, or when is this dispensation going to end and all that – when God has already revealed to us a pretty good bit of his knowledge. So, then, the Word must always be becoming flesh. The process of translation must always be taking place. You must take it from the printed page and make it flesh – your flesh – that the Word might dwell among you and that they might see it, see it in you as it glows among you, and give glory to the Father who is in heaven.

4

White Southern Christians and Race

In 1941, more than a decade before the civil rights movement would grab headlines, twenty-nine-year-old Clarence Jordan issued this challenge in the Baptist Student *magazine, a publication of the Southern Baptist Convention.*

IN FACING THIS NEW DAY and making the adjustments which it will usher in, the South must face very frankly and courageously several fundamental facts. In the first place, it must be willing to admit that there is no such thing as the inherent superiority or inferiority of races. Too frequently we Southerners have heard and even made the statement, "The Negro is all right in his place." And we have defined his place as that of servile inferiority. Politicians have been elected by overwhelming majorities on platforms of "white supremacy." We have told the Negro that this is a white man's country, and we have not even been embarrassed when he has asked in reply, "But did not the whites take it away from the red man?"

I believe that there are three very good reasons why the intelligent Christian cannot retain the position that one race is superior or inferior to another. First, the penetrating eye of science has not been able to see anything in the human race to justify placing a blue ribbon upon any branch of it. Biologists agree on the essential similarity of human bodies the earth over and the relatively superficial differences among them. Anthropologists have observed the striking psychic similarities among all people, their community of passion, action, and behavior patterns. Sociologists have discovered that one race will take on readily and easily the social characteristics of another. From the purely scientific standpoint, then, we might well suspect that Southern tradition has been guilty of error.

But there is a second reason of even greater importance, especially to those who profess to be followers of Jesus Christ. Nowhere in all the scriptures can there be supported the notion that God has favorite children. True, the children of Israel are regarded as God's chosen people, but they were chosen not simply for their own sake but to be a blessing to all people. At the very beginning of the Jewish nation, God incorporated all humankind in his covenant with Abraham. "In thee shall all families of the earth be blessed" (Gen. 12:3). When Jonah, a narrow Jew, obeyed God and preached to a city of hated Gentiles, God gave the greatest revival recorded anywhere in the Old Testament.

In the New Testament we fail to find any instance where Jesus allowed himself to be swept along with the prevailing currents of racial antipathy. He rebuked no other group so severely as the Pharisees, whose very name in the Hebrew means "separator," one who separates oneself from others. The Master also took great pains to show the folly of racial hatred between Jew and Samaritan. When other Jews, in going from Judea to Galilee, crossed the Jordan River and went completely around Samaria to avoid contact with its inhabitants, Jesus "must needs go through Samaria" (John 4:4). On another occasion, when he and his disciples were going through the land so despised by his countrymen, the Samaritans threw rocks at them. James and John wanted to solve the race question by calling down fire from heaven, but Jesus rebuked the sons of Zebedee and went on to the next village. And the beautiful and classic parable of the good Samaritan was told to a Jewish lawyer who tempted Jesus with the question, "Who is my neighbor?" (Luke 10:29–37). But the final stone in the wall of partition was removed when he commanded, "Go ye into all the world and preach the gospel to every creature" (Mark 16:15).

After his ascension, his disciples went everywhere and preached the Word. Philip could now sit down beside an Ethiopian. Peter could eat with Gentiles. And Paul, the Hebrew of the Hebrews, could say, "For there is no distinction between Jew and Greek: for the same Lord is Lord of all, and is rich unto all who call upon him; for, whosoever shall call upon the name of the Lord shall be saved" (Rom. 10:12). Thus, the serious Christian is faced with the question, "Shall the traditions of the world, or the teachings of Jesus Christ, dictate my attitudes and conduct?"

A third reason why one race should not consider the other race inferior is that differences cannot always be interpreted as deficiencies. We readily admit that the white and black races differ in many ways other than color of skin. But who can say that these distinguishing traits entitle either race to a claim of superiority? . . .

The eyes of the world are upon us. If we fail to get along with our black brothers and sisters, how can we honestly send missionaries to other peoples to proclaim the "Way"? . . . Young Christians, will you allow the Master whom you love thus to be humiliated? Is it not of grave concern to you that our conduct repudiates our belief? . . . And yet that is just what we are doing. All kinds of racial discriminations and injustices exist, yet scarcely a prophet raises his voice. Where are those daring youths who sing, "Where He Leads Me I Will Follow"?

5

No Promised Land without the Wilderness

Clarence Jordan was a trained Bible scholar who published his own colloquial translations. Here, in a snippet from a lecture series, we hear him expound on Exodus. Clearly, he could personally relate to Moses leading his people from the security of the familiar into the unknown.

"AND MOSES LED ISRAEL ONWARD from the Red Sea, and they went out into the wilderness of Shur, and they were in the wilderness three days and they found no water" (Exod. 15:22). In reality this narrative actually hurries on, condensing a great deal of experience into one brief verse. And the mood expressed in the words has changed from that so vividly reflected in the preceding poem. Obviously, the great moment has passed. The emotional apex of their experiences as they went out of Egypt – heightened to fever pitch when the pursuing legions fell short of overtaking them, only to perish in the attempt – had gone by. The spine-tingling thrill of escaping disaster subsided now that escape had been achieved. To put it colloquially, the group blood pressure went down to normal or even lower as they faced forward. Deliverance and survival inevitably compelled them to look ahead. As Egypt, darkness, and danger receded, their eyes turned of necessity in the opposite direction. For Israel, it was (as it is for anyone) a sobering experience. The prospect before them seemed bleak indeed. It was their own mysterious, indefinite, unpredictable, and uncharted future. The biblical phrasing of their predicament is fortunate in itself: "Onward from the Red Sea they went out into the wilderness." It was their success that created their problem. As for everyone else, so for them: the first stop on freedom's road is always the wilderness with its uncertainty and foreboding.

It is true of any road uphill that leads beyond the plateau of what is obvious and clear, or of any program that transcends the familiar and the habitual, that the fateful next step off beyond where one has hitherto stood, even to get away from whatever unsatisfactory present one may be involved in, automatically calls for reappraisal of one's situation. Any step forward, spiritually, always opens out upon vistas where the entire terrain may appear to be new and unfamiliar. Life takes on aspects never seen before. Living becomes bewildering in new ways and in different places. And the strangeness is due to having taken steps upward and forward. Therefore, the next thing after having done anything significant is the wilderness. To escape from the things that hold one down, to improve on what one has been doing, or to shake off the shackles that inhibit and constrain one's thinking and acting with courage in the name of an idea, and to follow some new beacon means problems that constantly clamor for attention. Only a short distance and a brief time, often just a few weeks or even days, and one is confronted with a totally new situation.

And if the leadership of any such forward-looking venture does not know in advance that this will be true, then all those participating in the enterprise are in for a bad time indeed. The Israelites might well have stayed in Egypt and enjoyed their leeks and their onions instead of venturing forth into the wilderness had not Moses, their leader, known and understood that brave action and high thinking bring on their own brand of consequences and that their early aftermath was bound to include uncertainty, bewilderment, hardship, and distress. With work and weariness, they would need to reshape their own world, even physically, to make a home within it for their future. As it is, the world about us is never automatically friendly to change or innovations, particularly in the realm of the spirit. It is never ready to welcome our developing idealisms. At the very best it expects, when we take a stand higher than the average, when our plans go beyond our hitherto best, that the results we hope for be guaranteed and even demonstrated beforehand. Moses was the kind of man that understood such things ahead of time. He knew that when one treads new territory, or advances beyond the familiar milestones, even if one goes in the name of God, the first thing encountered is predicament and then more predicament.

The Old Testament dramatizes Israel's wanderings in the wilderness realistically enough on the food-and-water level. Very soon they run out of food; soon they have no water that is drinkable. Each time that such a new bewildering problem faces the masses who follow the leader, the new predicament brings them in droves to complain to the leader; so Moses had to make good again and again. His role necessarily is cast in emergency and he becomes a twenty-four-hour coach to everybody on all sorts of problems. And problems are the only things he can be sure of or predict as their future in the wilderness unfolds.

When one has problems and they come thick and fast, they are likely to make one irritable; otherwise people generally enjoy problems, especially if they come singly or are reasonably spaced. Under such manageable conditions, one can play with them one at a time and feel imaginative and creative and keep working away on them at leisure. But when they crowd in because one has taken a courageous stand on a burning issue or a vital program, then one is prone to become irritable. As we read, not only in this passage but in dozens like it, "The people murmured against Moses, saying what shall we eat; what shall we drink?" Of course, it is commonplace to say that leadership which is never murmured against is hardly worthwhile. Nevertheless, we do well to remind ourselves that significant leadership, the kind of pastoral nurturing that a man practices with his flock, had better anticipate and figure on the times when the flock is likely to become irritable with the leader. For if a congregation is never aroused or disturbed, its leader can be reasonably certain that his program has not advanced very far beyond their average horizon. Moses gets more than his share of criticism and popular resentment. It usually comes in volume.

But the serious pursuit of a goal so high demands nothing less than tireless effort on the part of a leader, and, of course, eventual cooperation on the part of others also. Yet that kind of horizon in a world and time in which the ideal toward which he is striving has not yet caught on or found adherents is sufficient to test a man's stick-to-it-iveness as nothing else can.

This then is the perennial theme of the story of Moses' career, the sum and substance of the meaning of his work for his people. Spelled out, the road he persistently followed was uncharted. To begin with at least, it headed straight for the wilderness. No promised land was immediately available. Promised lands of any kind are not so much places ready-made and waiting to be occupied; they are essentially institutions to be painstakingly and eventually achieved by folk who have acquired the feel of the preliminary wilderness and who have had some practice in pioneering and in conceiving and constituting new institutions to implement a new and higher way of life. Thus Moses was a man who took people from one fresh vista to the next, never content to stop long at mere way-stations, nor ever satisfied to settle permanently at intermediate points, no matter how attractive or relaxing they might have been.

6

The Ten Commandments

The following six chapters are abridged from a series of talks Clarence Jordan gave to students at Goshen College in Indiana during 1965. Here he shows why the Ten Commandments still matter today.

IN ALL OF GOD'S DEALINGS with humankind, there have been two great outbursts, as though they were flares from the sun, when God could hardly hold himself back from breaking through to humankind. Both of these events in all of their brilliance took place on hilltops. Never has God spoken so brilliantly, so lovingly, so movingly, so understandingly as when he spoke to us through his dying Son on the hill of Calvary. Never before had God moved into human experience as he did on that little hilltop in an obscure, remote province of the Greco-Roman world two thousand years ago.

There is one other hilltop on which God tried to break through to man preceding that one. It was when God stood on the mountaintop of Sinai and spoke through Moses. Because of the magnificence and the transcendence of the event at Calvary, we sometimes let Sinai become overshadowed, and we relegate it to a position of unimportance. I want to revive it, to remind you that the utterances from Sinai have not been repealed nor abrogated. They are still very much in effect. My topic here is the Ten Commandments. This is a rather bad subject to talk to college students on because we don't like to hear dos and don'ts and we are inclined to think that this is a bit of unscientific literature gathered together from a rather obscure Code of Hammurabi.

"And God spake all these words." The author of these commandments is, according to the records, God himself. Now, it isn't just a God whom we might be afraid of, who is flashing lightning and thunder from the smoking mountains. He tells us who he is. He says, "I am the Lord God who hast brought thee out of the land of Egypt; out of the house of bondage" (Exod. 20:1–2).

The motive of the Ten Commandments is not fear, but love. I used to think that they were just great threats that God made to get us little kids to behave. I looked on them somewhat like my dad. He was a very strict person and I always thought that many of his orders were given largely because he would watch us to see if we would break them so he would feel perfectly justified and righteous in using the switch on us. He came from the old school of "spare the rod and spoil the child," and he didn't want to have any spoiled children running around his place. He had a number of boys – eight of us in all – and he used to tell the neighbors that whenever a new baby boy was born, he always planted a peach tree to raise him on. I didn't know for a long time that a peach tree ever had anything on it but switches. I asked my daddy one time where my peach tree was, and he said, "Son, yours died in its infancy from over-pruning." Well, God is not just giving us some orders so he can watch us to see whether we have disobeyed them so he will be perfectly justified in sending us to hell. That is not the motivation back of this. The motivation is love.

Another thing I want to point out before going into the text is that these are commandments; they are not suggestions. They are laws. There is a difference between a law and a suggestion. The law of momentum says that an object tends to go in a straight line in proportion to its mass and speed. If you get out here and get your speed up with enough weight behind you in an automobile, the law of momentum is going to close in on you and wrap you around a tree. You don't break the law of gravity. You just illustrate it. It breaks you.

Now, the Ten Commandments are great spiritual laws which are revealed to us out of God's love. When the Greeks gave a name to this magnificent universe of ours, they called it "cosmos," which means an orderly arrangement of affairs. When they looked out and saw the magnificent precision in the movement of the stars, the moon, the sun, the earth, when they saw in all of nature the precision with which everything was put together, they called it the cosmos. They saw the operation of the physical universe going according to precise, definite, infinitesimally carefully planned laws. When they looked into the realm of the mind, they found the same thing happening. Now, would it not be absurd to find a world of delicate order in the physical world, and to find things operating according to law in the mental world, and then find chaos and confusion in the realm of the spirit? It would not seem likely. The realm of the spirit is also governed by very definite laws. God in his great kindness drew back the curtain of the spiritual universe and let us catch a glimpse of what that spiritual order is like so that we might cooperate with it and live, and not rebel against it and die.

SO, WHAT DOES HE SAY? "I am the Lord thy God who hast brought thee out of the land of Egypt; out of the house of bondage. Thou shalt have no other gods before me" (Exod. 20:1–3). This is a commandment to two things. First, to monotheism – that God alone is God. This was the great contribution of the Hebrew people. Everywhere, no matter where they went, into captivity, up and down in their journeys, always it was the same: "Hear, O Israel, the Lord thy God is one God" (Deut. 6:4). Why were these Hebrew people obsessed with the unity of God, when all about them they saw fragmentation? I think they were concerned with the unity of God because they were concerned with the unity of life. Now, the old Greeks were very proficient in analyzing, fragmentizing, dissecting, pulling apart life and the universe. They cut it up into little, tiny fragments and cut it still further and further. On down and down they analyzed it. The Greeks were the great analysts, the great dissectors. But the Hebrews were the great unifiers. The Hebrews did not divide the man up into body, mind, and soul. He was just a man. So when all the rest of the world was trying to pick the world to pieces, the Hebrews were trying to put it back together. They saw life as one great whole with one great overarching God over everything.

I think this has tremendous significance to our culture today, when we are pursuing the path of the Greeks rather than the path of Hebrews. Our life is becoming increasingly fragmentized, even in our college studies. We are having to choose specialized fields, and then on down into subsections under that, and subsections under subsections under subsections of that, until finally, we just get to see a little gnat's-eye view of the universe. We become dwarfed little souls entombed in our tiny little compartments of life. And since we live in a little tiny tomb of life, we have to have us a little god over that little fragment of life. And so we have become, in many ways, like the Greeks. We have become polytheists rather than monotheists.

The other part of this law speaks not only to the fact that God is one, but that this God is supreme. He will brook no opposition. He will have no contenders for his position of lordship. In other words, the Hebrews were saying that life is one and that it is governed by a centralized authority, that it cannot be ruled by conflicting interests. They knew that man's ultimate destiny revolved around what he gave his ultimate allegiance to. When he gave his allegiance to conflicting deities, his life would be torn apart. The Hebrews knew that life did not have dual controls. Only one could guide the destiny of history, and only one could guide the destiny of the individual. You shall have no other gods before him.

THE NEXT COMMANDMENT SAYS, "Thou shalt not make unto thee any graven image or any likeness of anything that is in the heaven above, or that is in the earth beneath, or that is in the water under the earth. Thou shalt not bow down thyself to them, nor serve them" (Exod. 20:4–6). This is the commandment against idolatry, and we might say, "Well, we have no idols in America." Let's look. "Thou shalt not make unto thee any graven image." What does a man do when he makes a graven image? He takes a bit of stone or wood or whatever he may be working with and he begins to project into that wood or stone his own image of deity. He makes God after his own ideas. In other words, he makes a god which he can control, that will be simply a projection of his own mind. Now the old Greeks broke life all up into parts, and they had a god of agriculture and they had a god of industry. They also had a god of learning, and a god of medicine, and a god of health. They had a god of sex and a god of wine and pleasure – they broke them all up. But always they made themselves a god which they could control. Never would they allow themselves to handle a god who would control them. Always, they could tell their deity what his place was and what he could do. They had no idea of letting a god dictate to them sobriety; they were going to continue in their drunkenness. What would you do with a god of sobriety around who was telling you to sober up? You can't have a god like that, so you make yourself a god of wine who will get drunk with you. Then, if you're not going to give up your sexual lust and licentiousness, do you have a god of purity who tells you straighten up and clean up? Oh no. You can't have that, so you get yourself a god of sex. And if you are all running off to war, you are not going to have a god of peace who tells you to love your fellowman, so you make a god of war who will tag along with you anytime you want to go out on a little escapade. And so we make ourselves gods of our own creation whom we can call on to put their blessing and their sanction on our little plans.

One time, about ninety-three carloads of Ku Klux Klansmen came out to Koinonia Farm. They formed a procession nearly a mile long. We didn't know what it was at first. Somebody saw this procession coming, a long procession of automobiles creeping along, and when it got to our driveway, somebody said, "What is this? A funeral?" And a fellow stuck his head out the window and said, "Yeah, *yours!*"

Well, when the Ku Klux Klan got there, things were quite a good bit tense. They suggested that we find a climate a little bit more conducive to our health, and we were quite open to their suggestions at the time, but did not feel ourselves clear to make such a move. We learned later that before this Klan came out to Koinonia Farm on their night ride, they met in Americus in a big mass rally which was opened with prayer by a Baptist preacher. We've got to have a god that will fit into our little mold of things. We want to create him after our own ideas. And so we make God a segregationist. We make him a militarist. But the thing we love most to make of God is a successful businessman. Aw, yeah, God is a God . . . who blesses us with great prosperity. And when we get our bank accounts just *fat*, then we know God has really blessed us. He has. We just got his name wrong. It isn't Jehovah, it's Mammon. The Greeks had a name for that too. The more money you made, the richer you got, the more profligate your life, the happier old Mammon would be, because you made him to get happy with you when your bank account got big. He was your little financial buddy. That's all he was.

So human beings have been very proficient in creating images, gods that we can control. And this is a commandment prohibiting that. It would say, "Be ye not conformed to this world, but be ye transformed by the renewal of your mind" (Rom. 12:2). We are not to create God after our own image; we are to let him make us in his image. Whenever we set aside his word and say, "Yeah, I know the word of God says that, but it isn't practical in our age. Jesus was living way back yonder, you know, in a day when life was simple. He got a few little simple people about him and he didn't know anything about the complicated problems of American life. If he had lived today, he would urge us to be existentialists so that we would be pragmatic and face up to the complicated problems of our day." And so we set God's word aside and try to make him conform to our preset ways of life. This is breaking the second commandment.

THE THIRD COMMANDMENT SAYS, "Thou shalt not take the name of the Lord thy God in vain, for the Lord will not hold him guiltless that taketh his name in vain" (Exod. 20:7). Now, I know Mennonites certainly

wouldn't take the name of the Lord in vain, so perhaps
I could skip this one and move on to something else.
We don't cuss, do we? But, my friends, that isn't what
this means. Not at all. It has nothing to do with cussing.
What does it mean, to take the name of the Lord in
vain? Well, these Hebrew people were wandering around
out there in the wilderness. They could not be called
Egyptians; they had left Egypt. They could not be called
Canaanites; they had not arrived in Canaan. They had no
name. Today we mostly call people by their geographical
or ethnic origin. I'm a Georgian. And we might even
go further and call them by the name of the city they
are from. I would be called an Americus-ian, I guess, or
something of that nature. But back in those days, people
were called not by the nation or city from which they
came; they were called by the name of the deity which
they bore.

We even do the same today. People who follow
the teachings of Confucius are called Confucianists.
People who follow the teachings of Buddha are called
Buddhists. They take the name of Buddha. People who
follow Muhammad, they are called Muhammadans.
People who follow Christ, they are called Christians. So
to take the name means to take the name of the deity,

to say, "Yes, I am in that fellowship. I belong to it." Now, you cannot take the name of the deity in vain, or for nothing, unless first you take it. I can't take the name of Buddha in vain. I can get out on the street corner in front of the drugstore and say "Buddha damn" all night and not take Buddha's name in vain. I am not a Buddhist. I've never taken his name. So, since I have not taken his name, I can't take it in vain. A person who has never come within the Christian fold can't take the name of Christ in vain. He's never taken it. A Buddhist can't take the name of Christ in vain, no matter what one says. Only those who come within the church, who take on the name of Christ, can take his name in vain.

Now, you do not do it with your lips; you do it with your life. It is not the people on the outside of the church who take his name in vain saying naughty words. It's the people on the inside who say, "Yes, we are Christians," and then live as though Christ had never lived. What do we call that? We call it hypocrisy. Hypocrisy is taking the name of the Lord in vain, giving it out that you are walking under his name, but it means nothing to you. I remember when I was in high school. I came in late one night. I had been running around a good bit and my daddy had been looking for an opportunity to exercise his parental prerogative in turning me over his knee. Well, I remember I came in late and Dad called me into the living room. He said, "Son, I want to talk with you." I have forgotten nearly everything he said but one thing. Somewhere in the conversation he said, "Son, I have given you my name. I want you to keep it clean." Well, my father was saying the same thing to me that the Heavenly Father is saying to us in this third commandment. "My child, I've given you my name. Don't take it in vain. Keep it clean. Let it mean something when you are called a Christian. Don't let my name fall into disrepute because of you."

THE NEXT COMMANDMENT IS "Remember the Sabbath day to keep it holy. Six days shalt thou labor and do all thy work. But the seventh is the Sabbath unto the Lord thy God. In it, thou shalt not do any work" (Exod. 20:8–10). This commandment culminates the commandments dealing with our relationship to God. The first four deal with our loyalty to God; the last six deal with our relationship to people. I will not deal with the latter half of them. They are all summed up in, "Thou shalt love the Lord thy God with all thy heart and mind and soul and thy neighbor as thyself" (Matt. 22:37–39).

"Remember the Sabbath day to keep it holy." What does this mean? Well, the Hebrews struggled with this. They tried to decide what was the Sabbath day, and they finally decided that it was from sundown Friday until sundown Saturday. The problem they had, though, was determining what was work. Some of you, I'm sure, have read some of the old sayings in the Talmud in which they tried to spell out just what work was.

But this commandment really does not concern itself with either a day or with work. I think this is a symbol, a complete cycle of rest and work, seven days completing the whole cycle of life in which God is saying, "You ought to live and work." And don't forget that "six days thou shalt labor" is as much a part of the commandment as "one day shalt thou rest." It is the whole cycle of life that must be lived under God. Whether we rest, whether we work, the whole of life must be God's. There can be no segment of it left out.

The Christian interpretation of this is that the Sabbath rest was a whole way of life into which people moved, and they equated it with the kingdom of God. The Sabbath is not a day which you keep, it's that which you enter. It's not a day, it's a way. It's a kind of life. It's the kingdom of heaven. And when we enter it, not for just a few moments but for keeps, all work, whether it's on Saturday or Sunday, becomes worship. And God becomes our God and we become his children, and there is no more weeping nor crying, there is no more striving nor fighting. We have entered into our rest. We don't keep the Sabbath; it keeps us. We don't observe it; we live in it. Let us not, like those who had no faith, shrink back from this glorious movement which God has provided for us. But let us, through faith, move on in believing that God can create here on this earth his kingdom as it is in heaven.

7

Jesus, Leader of the Poor

*Here Clarence Jordan draws parallels between Jesus'
entrance into Jerusalem on Palm Sunday and Martin
Luther King Jr.'s recent March on Washington for Jobs and
Freedom.*

MANY OF us have a picture of Jesus that we gather from
the stained-glass windows, of a very delicate, effeminate
fellow. Sometimes we get an image of him from pictures
in our Bibles. I remember when I was a kid growing up,
my mother gave me an illustrated Bible, and my early
images of Jesus were born from that Bible. I saw him as
the good shepherd, walking along with a little lamb in
his arms and a pretty little staff in his hand, with daisies
tickling his toes and even his toenails well-manicured.
And long, beautiful, golden, auburn hair falling down
on his neck, all nicely fixed up as though he had just had
a Head & Shoulders shampoo! I almost thought that

he was a woman – he seemed so pretty, so nice, so well-manicured, his robe so clean and spotless.

I don't think this is the right picture of Jesus. I think he must have been a terrific *man!* One of the reasons he could command the respect of a rough fisherman like Simon Peter was that Jesus could beat him at fishing. I think if we had tried to follow Jesus around on some of his journeys, it would have worn most of us out. You had better take along some Sloan's Liniment – you would need it at the end of the day! And a man who can preach to five thousand men out in the open air without a microphone – he's got to have some lung power. I think when Jesus spoke his voice was as the roll of thunder. I've had enough public speaking to know you have got to have a pretty healthy diaphragm to get out that kind of thunder.

Jesus was a man, a man among men, and more than that, he was the leader of a revolutionary movement. The reason I think that is because he led a great mass demonstration on one occasion. We think Martin Luther King invented the mass demonstration method. No, it wasn't original with Martin Luther King – Jesus put on a big one! (I don't know who did invent it; I don't think Jesus did, but he certainly knew how to put on a mass demonstration.) He identified himself with the poor people, not just of one race but of all races, and he wanted to demonstrate in the capital city of his land the rights of the poor people. So he gathered together a great crowd of these poor people and then told his disciples he was going to lead the demonstration. He said, "I need something to ride on." Now, this is interesting! Anyone who is going to enter the city as the king usually gets himself a big, white Arabian steed. We would expect Jesus to say, "You all go up to Tyre or Nineveh and get me one of those fine Arabian stallions – I want to do this thing up right!" But do you know what he said to his disciples? "I want you to go into the village there and get me a mule." And he said, "I want you to get me one on which no one has ever sat" (Mark 11:2). Now Jesus must have been a real man to ask for that kind of mule! I tried once to sit on "a mule whereon no man had ever sat" and when I got through with him he was still "a mule whereon no man had ever sat!" But Jesus could ride that mule. The mule was the symbol of the lowly, the working classes, the toiling people. And I know what it means to be behind one of those hay-burners myself. I plowed with them and I want to say that a slow mule and a hot sun

has called many a man into the ministry! That's why the
South produces so many preachers, I think.

Well, this was a symbol of the lowly people, and Jesus
was leading a mass demonstration, identifying himself
with these people. And you know, people said to him the
same thing they say to people who lead mass demonstrations today. When he started into the city on his mule
and all those people started waving branches – heaven
knows that's enough to scare a mule to death! I don't see
how he could have ridden a *tame* mule, with everybody
waving those palm branches and throwing their shirts
and hollering, "Hosanna, Hosanna to the King of
David!" I don't see how he ever controlled that animal,
but he did, and rode on through.

And the big, old leaders, the mayor and the chief of
police, came out to him and said, "Tell your folks to shut
up! They are parading without a permit!" And Jesus said,
"If I tell these people to hush, the very stones will cry
out!" (Luke 19:40). When you tell the throbbing, seeth-
ing masses to stop their revolution, to go back home and
be content – when the ferment is brewing you can't stop
that kind of a revolution and Jesus knew it. The leaders
said, "We don't want outside agitators coming in here

and stirring up our good content black folk. Get them out and go back home!" Jesus said, "If I tell them to hush even the rocks will pick up the chorus and start crying out for the poor!"

8

Love Your Enemies

BEYOND ALL DOUBT, the most vexing problem, from prehistoric times to the present, has not been how to pass a final examination, get a degree and a high salaried job, marry a beautiful girl and get a slick car and live in a swank house in the suburbs. Those problems are but trivial in comparison to the problem of learning how to respond maturely to those who oppose us. We have learned how to respond to our friends. But to respond to our enemies, ah, that is the problem! How can we be mature? How can we make a grown-up response to people who want to do us in, to hound us, to beat us, to persecute us?

We would expect our Lord to be quite clear in his teachings on this subject, and he was (Matt. 5:38–45). He begins by going deep into history and digging up various responses that people have made. All of us respond in one of four ways:

1. One is the method of *unlimited retaliation.* If somebody knocks out your eye, you knock out *both* of his. If somebody knocks out your tooth, you knock all his teeth out (if you can get to him). If somebody kills your dog, you kill his cow; if he kills your cow, you kill his mule; if he kills your mule, you kill him! No limit to the amount of retaliation: unbridled anger, unbridled vengeance.

Humankind seems to have outgrown this idea early on, but has lapsed back into it with the invention of the atomic bomb. This seems to be the principle which dominates the state departments of most so-called civilized nations: "You bomb us, we will obliterate you. You bomb a little city, we will annihilate a whole nation." Unlimited, massive retaliation. Now this was so childish, so barbaric, so beastly that it never occurred to our Lord that anyone within his hearing would ever resort to it – I guess he just didn't know twentieth-century man.

2. Jesus picked it up there and said, "Now wait, if some-body knocks out your eye, don't knock both of his eyes out." The old prophet, Moses, said, "One eye for an eye, one tooth for a tooth." If he knocks out your eye, don't knock out both his eyes, just knock out one. If he knocks

out your tooth, don't knock out all of his teeth, just knock out one tooth. This was the first effort at *restraint on the strong.* Now Jesus says, "Moses gave you that idea, but it is not enough; let us move on up to another one.

3. And so the old prophet came along and said, "Love your neighbor and hate your enemy." This was the first glimmerings of *limited* love. If your neighbor knocks out your tooth, forgive him; but if he is a person of another race or another nation, give him the works. In other words, limit your love to your own little group, your own nation, your own race. This is the rule of limited love.

This concept enables people to live together as a nation, limiting their love to their own nation, but it does not enable them to live together as a world family. Now, this seems to be the place that most of us really are today. We love America, and limit our love to the shores and boundaries of the United States. I think most of us reflect the idea that is inscribed on an old tombstone down in Mississippi: "Here lies John Henry Simpson. In his lifetime he killed 99 Indians and lived in the blessed hope of making it 100 until he fell asleep in the arms of Jesus." Indians didn't count; you could kill ninety-nine of them and live "in the blessed hope" of getting just one more to round it out in an even hundred and still "fall asleep in the arms of Jesus." But if you had killed just one white person, you would fall asleep in a noose.

A nation can drop an atomic bomb on "other people" and annihilate two whole *cities* of people and we give the pilot a medal. If he kills one person in the United States, we give him the electric chair. "Love your neighbor, those of your own race, your own group."

Down in Georgia some kids working in the civil rights movement ran out of gas. They were an integrated group. They were out in the country and two of the white ones decided to go for some gas. They came to a farmer and he got them out a gallon of gas and said, "Where's your car?"

They said, "About a mile up the road."

He said, "Well, get in. I'll take you up there."

And they said "No, we . . . we'll just walk."

He said, "Why, no, it's too hot. I wouldn't think of letting you walk. Get in."

"No," they said, "we'd rather walk. We need the exercise."

But he said, "No, it's too hot. Come on, get in, I'll take you up there." So very reluctantly the two white kids got in with this white farmer. They drove along and finally he said, "Where's your car?"

They said, "There it is, right over there." So they stopped and got out and the farmer realized that it was some of those integrationists. He became infuriated! He grabbed his can, put it back in the car, and drove off in a huff. If they had been all white, he would have been a fine Southern gentleman, a deacon in the Baptist church, "asleep in the arms of Jesus." But now he is dealing with people of a different race, and he cannot love *those* people.

4. Jesus said it is not enough to limit your love to your own nation, your own race, your own group. You must respond with love even to those outside of it, and respond with love to those who hate you. This concept enables human beings to live together, not just as nations but as the human race. We are now at the stage of history where we will either take this step or perish. For we have learned with consummate skill how to destroy humankind. We have learned how to efficiently annihilate the human race. But somehow or other, we shrink with horror from the prospect, not of annihilation, but of reconciliation. We shall either be reconciled, we shall either love one another, or we shall perish.

Now, Jesus did not advocate nonviolence. He was not advocating passive resistance. He does not say, "If your enemy slaps you on the right cheek, put on a demonstration protesting your right to preserve at least the rouge on that particular cheek." He is not commanding us to demand our rights. The only right that love has is the right to give itself.

At times, this may be passive; that is, you may do nothing to a person who opposes you. I was at the Sumter County livestock sale sometime back, buying some calves that we needed at the farm. I bought them and was just about ready to leave when the town's arch-segregationist came in. Well, I didn't want to have a consultation with him at that moment. I kind of shrunk down behind everyone else and looked for a mouse hole, but I couldn't find one. Finally, he came in and looked around and saw me. He came over and stood about two or three feet in front of me and yelled at the top of his voice, even above the noise of the auctioneer, "Here's that old Jordan fellow, folks! We ain't killed him yet, but we can kill him now. We got him here by himself!" I started looking for even a knothole to get through, but couldn't find one. Then he looked at me and raised his voice again and said, "You ain't nothing but a . . ." – he made a positive statement that on my mama's side I had some canine ancestry. Now, down where I come from, when someone attributes to you that kind of a pedigree, you are supposed to respond. And I felt my fist getting in a position to respond. And then he took a deeper breath and called me something else, and I noticed that while he didn't have any teeth he did have tonsils. And I thought this would be a nice time to perform a public tonsillectomy! But somehow God gave me the power to restrain myself. The little fellow kept calling me increasingly long names. I did not know there were that many species around until he called me those names. Well, he finally gave up and went outside.

There was a big, two-hundred-pound farmer sitting next to me. Every time the little fellow would call me one of those names, this farmer would grimace. Finally he said, "You know what?" And I thought he was getting ready to take up where the little fellow had just left off.

I said, "What?"

He said, "I want to know how come you didn't hit that little fellow? You could have really whooped him, with one arm tied behind your back."

I said, "I think that is a correct appraisal of the situation."

He said, "Well, how come you didn't hit him?"

I said, "My friend, there are two reasons why I didn't

hit him. One is purely selfish. If I had hit that little segregationist, everybody in this sale barn would have jumped on me and *mopped up* the floor with me, and I just didn't want my wife married to a mop. But the real reason is that I am trying to be a follower of Jesus Christ, and he has taught me to love my enemies." I said, "Now, while I must confess I had the minimum amount of love for this little fellow at the time, at least I did him no harm."

And this old fellow said, "Is *that* what it means to be a Christian?"

I said, "Friend, that is not all it means, but that is a part of it." We sat for a while, talking about being a Christian.

It is not enough merely to not harm our enemies. Somehow or another, we must go beyond that. Love is not merely a weapon. It is not a strategy, and it may or may not work. To do good to those who hate you is such stupendous folly that it cannot be expected to work. Love didn't work for Jesus. No one has ever loved as he loved, but it didn't work, even for him. He wound up on a cross.

And yet it *does* work, if your motive is not to *make* it work. Love works in the home, but if you say, "It really works to love your wife; if you love her, she will darn your socks and bake you a pie every day" – if that is the

motive for love, I doubt your wife will darn your socks
and bake you pies. But love does work. I think Abraham
Lincoln said it so well. After the war was over there was
much sentiment in the North to just crush the South.
Thaddeus Stevens, a very bitter man from the North
who was in the Cabinet, shared this viewpoint. One
day, when Mr. Lincoln was advocating binding up the
wounds of the nation, forgiveness, and reconciliation,
Thaddeus Stevens pounded the table and said, "Mr.
Lincoln, I think enemies ought to be destroyed!"

Mr. Lincoln quietly said, "Mr. Stevens, do I not
destroy my enemy when I make him my friend?"

In the long run, it is the only way that really does
work. For when the cards are all in, and the final chapter
of history is written, when time is rolled up as a garment,
and God is all and in all – on that final day it will be the
peacemakers, not the warriors, who will be called the
children of God.

9

Jesus and Possessions

I HAVE SPENT a good bit of time on various college campuses, and one thing I notice on every college campus is that everybody seems to be in a hurry. Everybody is in a rush. Everybody is trying to get something and when you quiz them a little further, you find that they are out to get a good grade. They are thinking about examination day and thinking about those report cards that will go back home. If you ask them, "Why are you so concerned about your grades?" they will give you some tommyrot about how they want to please their mama and daddy. But if you really get them to tell you the truth, they will tell you, "I want to get good grades because I know when I get out of here, the big jobs will go to those in the upper percentage of the class. And I want the big job, and I want the big money."

Now, how does all this stack up with the mind of Jesus? We think of Jesus as poor. He owned no land, he had no house, he had no furniture, he had no automobile – not even a yoke of oxen. In fact, to use his own words, he had nowhere to lay his head – or we would say, nowhere to hang his hat. He had no bank account, no insurance, and – you will not believe this – he didn't even have a Social Security number. By Western standards, he was a penniless tramp – at best, a high-minded hobo. Most of us would have been embarrassed to have had him in our fashionable homes, and we would have been ashamed to acknowledge him as our friend. The most educated and successful among us would have given him some free lectures on getting ahold of himself, settling down in a good job, raising a family, and a lot of other free pointers on successfully conforming and adjusting to modern life. Perhaps we would have gone so far as to offer our help in assisting him to make contact with certain influential leaders in the town, like Caiaphas, the high priest. "I know him; maybe he can get you a job over at the Temple." Or, "I know Pilate, the governor. He may be able to help you get a job with the Internal Revenue Service. I would be glad to put in a good word for you, Jesus, if you will just settle down and get ahold of yourself and quit all this tramping around all over the world talking to the people about the God movement."

We would have urged him, especially, to give up his messianic delusions and not to ruin himself and his future by taking such positive stands on controversial social issues.

But was Jesus really poor? We say he was and the scriptures seem to tell us he was, but was he *really* poor? If so, there is something fishy about the whole thing because he certainly didn't have to be poor. He was a preacher, he was a teacher, and he was a healer, or a doctor. Now, in his day, you could have been rather rich practicing any one of those three professions. Things have changed around a little bit today. One of them is still in the upper bracket, but in Jesus' day, you didn't have to do all three. You didn't have to moonlight. If you were that kind of a fellow with those kinds of skills, you could have been rich just preaching. You could have been rich teaching. You could have been rich healing. And Jesus was skilled in all three. You tell me he was poor? With his preaching, he could attract Billy Graham crowds. You think he couldn't pass the collection plate when he had that many folks out there? With his teaching, he was a one-man university. And with his healing, he outdid the Mayo Clinic and Oral Roberts combined. How much were the free-will offerings at his evangelistic crusades? What were his matriculation fees for his classes? I have had kids in college enough to know that matriculation fees come pretty high these days. Suppose it were announced that tomorrow night the Master himself would give a lecture in this hall, and he would give the original lecture of the Sermon on the Mount. We are going to charge ten dollars for admission. I venture to say this place would be packed to the gills. Jesus could have gotten a pretty big sum out of the gate receipts. What were his charges for professional services when he healed the lepers, gave sight to the blind, and raised the dead? Come now, surely he had money stacked away by the sackful. He couldn't have helped it.

I think we can safely say he did not. I think he had absolutely nothing when he died. All he had on his back was a robe and that was his sole legacy. Well then, why? What was the matter with a fellow like that, so skilled, with such great talent, and dying a pauper? Wouldn't we say that a doctor who was a skilled surgeon would need his head examined if he didn't live out in the suburbs in a big house? Wouldn't we say something is wrong with the guy?

What is the matter with Jesus if he did not have great wealth? Well, I think he didn't have it, primarily, because he didn't want it. It wasn't that he could not have made it – he could have. It was just that he didn't want it. And he didn't want it for several good reasons. One, because of its perishability. He says worms and rust and thieves finally wind up getting ahold of it. What is the use of spending your life trying to get ahold of something that worms can beat you to, or rust can outdo you in getting ahold of, and thieves can dig through and get it even after you get it? Why spend your time chasing after those kinds of things? Why work yourself into the grave for things that worms can get better than you can? Sooner or later, the ravages of worms, rust, and thieves will plunder all wealth.

Sooner or later, in spite of all of our efforts, in spite of all of our safeguards, from burglar alarms to embalming, there is absolutely no protection against the perishability of those things that we set our hearts upon. It is somewhat like when a very wealthy man in the community died, somebody asked my brother: "Buddy, have you heard how much he left?" and Bud said, "No. I haven't, but I suppose he left it all." Give or take a few dollars, that is how much all of us leave.

I think, however, that Jesus did not want to set his heart upon wealth not only because of its perishability but also because of its possible effect on people. He could see that it could lead to addiction. Just as alcohol can lead to alcoholism, so money can lead to moneyism. It sets up a fever in the human breast, a craving. Now, I have had a lot of dealings with alcoholics and I have seen the burning in their eyes when you take their liquor away from them. I have seen the craving thirst on their lips. And I have seen the great lengths they will go to get alcohol when you take it away from them. But I will tell you truly, I have never seen alcoholics go to such great lengths to get liquor as people on Main Street will go to get money. It is a thirst, an addiction, which can crush and kill people. Many, many people who would think twice about getting drunk on alcohol will go on a big old greedy binge trying to buy up every piece of land they can get. Like the old farmer who, when they accused him of being greedy and wanting everybody's land, said, "I don't want everybody's land. All I want is just that land that adjoins mine." Now, we would turn a fellow out of our churches if he got drunk on liquor; but we will make a deacon out of him if he is drunk on money and tithes it.

Jesus saw that it was an addiction that blinded people, crushed them, and made them victims of it. Next, he saw that not only would it form an addiction – and I tell you it is a thirsty crave once you get it – not only that, it distorts a person's vision. It keeps a person from seeing clearly.

It distorts our vision, and then it makes a person awfully vulnerable. A person who has got a lot of money is really vulnerable to the temptations and the attacks of the evil one. This is true not only of an individual, but also of an organization. The real cutting edge of the civil rights movement was a student group in the South, SNCC [Student Nonviolent Coordinating Committee]. The reason for it is that college kids do not have any money, by and large, and these kids with no money to lose were able to give themselves to abandon. The older folks, both white and black, could hardly participate in it because they were vulnerable economically. Jesus did not want to be economically vulnerable. He wanted to be poor so that he could make his decisions clearly without any distortion of vision. Because Jesus wanted to see clearly, because he didn't want to be vulnerable, and because he wanted to deal justly and to walk humbly with his God, he was a pauper.

IO

Metamorphosis

THERE IS AN ANTICIPATION in the Gospels of a dawning new era, a great light arising. All those who have watched longingly and desperately through the long night watches now begin to see the glimmerings of a dawn. This is a time of great rejoicing, when all nature arises from its sleep and humanity itself comes to life.

This is a figurative way of saying that Jesus had come to usher in the dawn of a new movement – not a New Deal, but a new era, a whole new way of life. So then, from that time on, Jesus began to cry out and to say, "Change your way of living, for the kingdom of the Spirit is here," or "is upon you" (Matt. 4:17). He visualized his movement as being a dawning of this new era, but people had to get ready for it. It was a new day a-coming, but people could not enter into it as they were. Our English word "metamorphosis" comes from the Greek – *meta* meaning a change, *morpheus* meaning body or form.

The Greeks also had a word for change of attitudes, of inner life: *metanoia.* We do not have an English word that corresponds to that, a change of personality, of outlook, of mind – not a change but a transformation. I guess we would have to call this the metamorphosis of the soul or something of that nature. People are called upon to be prepared for a new order.

We know what metamorphosis is. Here is a little caterpillar crawling along in the dirt. He goes up on a little twig, maybe he spins a cocoon about himself. Then great forces of nature begin to prey upon him. The spring comes, the summons to the new order of the air besieges and besets that little cocoon, and out of it emerges, from that little ugly caterpillar, a beautiful monarch butterfly. There is the same essential nature in both the caterpillar in the cocoon and the butterfly, but they are made for different orders. One responds to the order of the dirt, the ground, the lower level. The other hears the call of the air, the perfume of the flowers, the beautiful array of the fields of flowers.

When nature begins to call to the little caterpillar to metamorphose, it is calling him to a new order; new things are at hand. Jesus visualized his movement as being a new order. Great things were in the making and he was calling Judaism to change its ways, to come out of its old hidebound traditions, to throw off the old yoke of bondage and come anew and enter into the new covenant relationship with God.

I realize what I am saying is rather abstract to you. It was abstract to Jesus. So he had to make it specific; he had to make it concrete. He said, "The new order of the Spirit is here," and everybody would say, "Where?" So he had to get something that he could point to, something specific. Now, Jesus' method was quite different from ours. We preachers take the simple and make it complicated. Jesus took the complicated and made it simple. He took the abstract and made it concrete.

Jesus was enough of a farmer to realize that he had to have something to experiment with, and then he had to demonstrate something. He had to have a demonstration plot to try out these great ideas of the kingdom – of the new order of the Spirit. Where was he going to get the people for this? He was going around, picking them out. Walking along beside the Sea of Galilee, he saw two brothers, Simon and Andrew, throwing their nets into the sea, for they were fishermen. And he said to them, "Y'all come with me . . ." (Matt. 4:19). And right away they left their nets and fell in behind him.

I think Jesus is building a little microcosm of the world, a sampling of society, picking fishermen. Next he picked a tax collector, a publican. Now, frankly, if I had been setting up a movement, I don't believe I would have chosen a Repub– uh, publican. These fellows were not popular. Nobody liked them. They collected taxes from the Jewish people and sent it off to the Roman government. He would be just about as popular in our part of the country as a fellow from the federal government trying to enforce integration. This publican was just hated. He was a collaborationist with the occupying forces. But Jesus chose him.

Then he chose another fellow by the name of Simon the Zealot. These Zealots were very interesting people; they were the super-duper patriots of Jesus' day. All you had to do was strike up one strain of Dixie and they would be out there waving the Confederate flag. They were all for it. Their motto was, "Save your Confederate money, boys, the South will rise again!"

In order to be a Zealot, you had to make an oath to three things. You said, one, "No tax but the temple tax." That is, you would pay the religious tax but you wouldn't pay the federal income tax. Second, "No lawgiver but Moses." You wouldn't take the decisions of the federal

Supreme Court; only Moses had the right to tell his
people what to do. And, third, "No king but Jehovah."
You wouldn't take the laws from the Roman emperor.
Now, one other thing you had to do when you became
a Zealot was to swear that if opportunity ever afforded
itself you would assassinate publicans. You had to look
for an opportunity, and if you ever found one where you
could get away with it, you would slit his throat.

So Jesus chose Matthew the publican and Simon the
Zealot, the absolute opposite extremes of society, and
put them in the same fellowship. Can you imagine it? I
venture to say that on more than one night, Jesus had
to sleep between those two boys. Poor old Matthew the
publican never knew when he might wake up in the
still wee hours of the night to find a cold piece of steel
on his throat. If Jesus could take a wild-eyed, fanatical,
patriotic Zealot and a celebrating publican and put them
in the same sack and shake them up and cause them to
have the love of God in their hearts so that they could
walk down Main Street in Jerusalem holding hands and
calling one another "Brother Matt" and "Brother Simon,"
the kingdom of God was *there.* It was absolute proof
that the reign of God had changed these people from
the little old caterpillars of hate and prejudice and greed

and had made them into the butterflies of his new order. When somebody would say, "Where is this kingdom of God you are talking about?" he could say, "Right there. There is Simon, there is Matthew. Here are the men that I have planted these ideas among, and here is the way it is expressing itself."

Jesus was seeking to experiment with these ideas; I don't think he really knew how they were going to come out. And, more than that, he was trying to demonstrate to the world that the new order of the Spirit was dawning. I think this is what God is always trying to do. The Word did not become flesh as a point in history. The incarnation is not a point. It is a process. The ideas of God are constantly struggling for expression in the experience of humanity. And before this new order can ever become a reality, it has got to take root in our own lives. Somewhere, we have got to build a fellowship where people are transformed from the old things, where the old things pass away and all things become new. Jesus is seeking constantly, throughout history, to project this. We cannot enter this new order with the old trappings. The caterpillar must lay aside its skin and its cocoon. We cannot enter the kingdom of peace with a six-shooter on our hip. We will never enter the kingdom of peace with atomic missiles aimed at the throat of our brother. We are going to have to restructure the whole thing. We will never enter into a kingdom of brotherhood with lines of segregation all about us. Our minds have to be changed and, in time, our structures will have to be changed.

So Jesus would be saying to us and to all, "Metamorphose! There's a new order, a new day, breaking."

II

The Man from Gadara

THE STORY of the man from Gadara (Mark 5:1–20) illustrates a truth, the truth that sooner or later all of us are caught in some kind of tremendous religious conflict and tension. None of us ever escapes it.

The man from Gadara was caught in a great, grinding conflict. Society was crushing him, trying to push him, to shape him, to conform to the mold which society had made for him. It is a long story. It occurs in all three of the synoptic Gospels, and we wonder why it was ever put in here because, on the surface, it is so meaningless. But when we dig deep into it, we see that no event in all of the life of Jesus so illuminated his great insight into social problems, into the predicament of people caught in conflicts, many times of their own making, and how our Lord saw through all of this and pointed to the way out and put the person back together again.

The setting of the story is the territory over just beyond the Sea of Galilee in Gentile territory. It is the region of the ten cities that were used by Pompey as military garrisons, outposts to guard the land of Palestine. Here lived people outside the covenant relationship to God. This is one of Jesus' rather few forays into foreign territory. He goes over into the land of Gadara, just across the Sea of Galilee. "And when he got out of the boat, right away, there met him, coming out of the tombs, a man with a dirty spirit – an unclean, filthy spirit – who has his dwelling place in the tombs." He had been bound with both leg chains and handcuffs, but he ripped them off of himself. Here we find a fellow whose life is in awful conflict, and the only answer that society is giving to this man in his terrible trouble is chains.

This man immediately gives the impression of estrangement. He cannot live in the city. He perhaps went there seeking anonymity and he got it – more than he expected. He finally just lost himself, and now he flees from the city and goes out into the tombs – loneliness, seeking in death, in the caves of death, some kind of fellowship, perhaps, symbolically identifying himself with the dead rather than the living. He is cut off from warm fellowship. It is as though he is a ghost, a disembodied, impersonal being, living in the tombs and cutting himself with rocks.

In the early beginnings of the Jewish nation when circumcision was given to them as a symbol, or the initiatory rite into the nation, into the family, the operation was performed with a stone. And when the male Jewish child was circumcised, it was at that point he became a member of the household of God. This was the sign of the covenant relationship. It was about the equivalent of baptism. Now, this fellow apparently feels that the covenant relationship has been broken. He is no longer a member of the household. He is excommunicated, he is in the land of the dead, and I wonder if, perhaps, he is not mutilating himself with the stones trying in some masochistic way to bring himself back into the fellowship. I think this cutting himself with the stones is an important thing to help us understand the psychological turmoil in this man's heart – yearning for restoration, for fellowship.

When the man saw Jesus, he ran up to him and said, "I am warning you, do not get me all riled up. Jesus, do not bring in any more of this God thing. Do not bring religion into my problem." Perhaps this man's problem had something to do with religion. Perhaps it was a warped concept of religion that had upset him and torn him and he is saying, "I've had enough of that stuff. Don't bring up the subject of religion with me again. I can't stand it." Now, Jesus doesn't press the point. He begins with this question, "What is your name?" And the man says, "My name is Legion, multitudes, for there are a lot of us." What is my name? I am no longer a name. I am a number. I have no name. I am nameless. I am impersonal. I am disembodied. But there are thousands of kids like me who haven't been able to make heads or tails of religion nor of life. And we are fed up with it! Just call us "Multitudes." Now, Jesus is trying to restore some measure of identity, some measure of personality into this man by saying to him: Think now, kid, think! You had a name! What is your name? You are a human being. Let's begin with that. We won't argue theology. We'll begin with the fact that you are still a human being.

"This multitude of spirits called out to Jesus and asked if they could enter a herd of nearby hogs. And Jesus agreed that they might go into them. So the spirits came out of the man and entered into the hogs. Then the whole herd rushed down the slope into the sea. There were about two thousand of them, and they drowned in the sea." I think these hogs might be the clue to the interpretation of the whole passage. What were these two thousand hogs doing just across the sea from Galilee where the Hebrews dwell who never had a reputation for eating hog meat? Why would anybody want to go down there and set up a hog-feeding establishment? That would be the last place in the world I would want to raise hogs, right next to a hog-dry country. The Jews did not eat country ham. What is this bunch doing right across the lake from them? Ah, maybe that is just it. Perhaps up north, in Galilee, those religious people were not the old orthodox, fundamentalist literalists that they were down in Judea. Up north, there in Galilee, they had become theologically liberal to the point that, every now and then, they would go to the little coffee house and get themselves a country ham sandwich. Nothing wrong with just eating a little country ham. The folks were liberal up there; but still, hog meat wasn't legal. It was black market hog meat. Now, is there a better place to raise hogs than right across the county line from where it is dry? That's where the bootleggers set up. These were bootleg hogs, black market hogs.

Where did this young man come from? I don't know. But unless I miss my guess, this young fellow is the man in the parable of the prodigal son (Luke 15:11–32). I think this is the prodigal son who said, "I want to go out in the world and see what things are like." He said, "How about divvying up and giving me my share of the business?" "Okay, son, we will do that." And so the young boy gets his share of the business, and he goes away into a far country. How far? Oh, maybe up north to some of the colleges up there. You all know what he did, he went up there to get an education. At least, he went a long way from his religious upbringing.

It says that when he got up there, his money began to give out and there were hard times in the land – the depression hit about that time – and this boy couldn't get a job, he didn't have a scholarship, his money was gone, and he needed some help. And so he goes out and gets a job with one of the citizens of that country who, perhaps, had a hog-feeding establishment right across the lake so he could bootleg it in over the Galilee.

Now, this kid had been taught that it was wrong to eat hog meat. All his life, he had been taught no really honest devout Jew would ever eat hog meat. This has been trained into him ever since he was a little bitsy fellow. You know how hard it was for Peter to eat his first meat when he was at the house of Simon the Tanner (Acts 10). The Lord had to let that tablecloth down three times with meat on it before he could finally get Peter to get up and cut himself off a big hunk of ham. It's hard for a fellow to go against his religious upbringing. Now, this young fellow knew it was wrong to eat hog meat. But here he is, now, with a job – not only eating hog meat, but raising them. You can imagine the tremendous turmoil in this boy's heart. Every time he went out there to throw slop to those hogs, he perhaps wondered, "Look what I am. Here I am, engaging in a shady business, contrary to the religion that my father and my mother taught me."

I imagine it was that hog-feeding escapade that finally broke the boy down. He could not stand it. His religious upbringing was clashing with terrific noise against the social environment in which he found himself. Here was society saying, "Aw, a little piece of ham, everybody eats a little ham every now and then, there is nothing wrong with it. A little nip of ham just before you go to bed is real nice. Everybody enjoys a little nip of ham. Nothing wrong with it." And then, on the other hand, all this intense religious training saying, "It's wrong to eat ham, it's wrong to eat ham," and here this boy is, caught in this big conflict. And he is feeding hogs because he himself is hungry – an economic necessity.

Jesus could never deal with this boy's problem unless he dealt with those hogs, for that is what had driven him crazy. He had just gone nuts over this problem of trying to reconcile his religious upbringing with his social environment. And Jesus could never straighten this boy out unless he went directly to the cause of his problem. So he says to those hogs, "Not only may you go, you *must* go."

This raises the question: "But two thousand hogs? That's a heap of hogs – a pretty good investment. Would the Lord allow that much waste of property?" We sometimes say, "Look. We got so much invested in our program, in our building, in all this kind of thing. Would the Lord smite it?" If economics gets in the way, if that is what is driving us, if that is what is killing us, of course he would. What are two thousand hogs when there is one soul involved? Suppose it had been your kid, going off to college and getting in with some of this wild philosophy that was pulling his mind apart, and it cost you your whole herd of two thousand hogs. Wouldn't you put it up? Of course you would. Jesus is saying economics must be subservient to the needs of people.

The people started flocking out there and "they see this man who was demon possessed now fully clothed and in his right mind." Where did the man get those clothes? There was no haberdashery close by. Here, a man was enfolded into the fellowship with Jesus and his disciples who shared their clothes with him, and for the first time in the man's life since he left his old father back home, he feels he is in the family. The loving fellowship surrounds this naked man and provides for his needs off their own backs. They put not only their arms around him, they put their shirts off of their backs around this wild lunatic. Now, the man knows what it means to be in the fellowship. Now he is in his right mind.

The people said, "Jesus, get away from here." He said, "All right, I'll go." And the man said, "I want to go with you. I want to help you preach the gospel. It's so wonderful to be in this fellowship, to be with brothers who will share the shirt off their backs. You don't know what it means to be a member, now, of the new Israel, to be brought into God's family. I want to stay in this." And Jesus perhaps said, "No, son. You've been away too long already. I think it is time you go on back to your father. You're in your right mind, now, you've come to yourself. How about going back home and letting your father see that you're in your right mind?" And the young man says, "I'll do it," and he gets up and goes home and is going to say, "Father, I am no more worthy to be called your son."

But the old father wouldn't hear of it. "Bring the robe, the fatted calf, the ring, the shoes. No, I won't hear of this servant business. You're my boy."

This is one of the most marvelous stories and it speaks to us many things. One thing it speaks to me is that you better be careful about what you teach your children to be the will of God. It would be better to never teach them anything at all about God than to teach them the word of God and then bring them up in a society that nullifies the whole thing. You want me to illustrate what I am talking about? One time, we had a fellow come to Koinonia from the mountains of North Carolina. He had been in the war. He had grown up in North Carolina, and he said that he had a very gentle mother who had taught him the word of God and had taught him gentleness. He told me, one time, that he couldn't even kill a chicken for dinner – that he just couldn't bring himself to killing a chicken. The war came along. Uncle Sam said, "I need *YOU!*" and picked him up, sent him to a boot camp, trained him in the art of murder, and sent him over across the sea. This boy killed a man. This boy, who had been taught by his mother such infinite kindness and gentleness that he couldn't even kill a chicken, was ordered to kill a man and he did it. It broke him. He came out a mental case. He went through the hands of many psychiatrists. Finally, he was released and he came to Koinonia.

Now, for quite some while, he would be in his right mind. He was perfectly normal, apparently. But every once in a while – we never had any warning of when it would be, sometimes in the night, sometimes in the day – this grown man would have this seizure of some kind. And he would just rip off every stitch of clothing that he had on him, just tear it off until he became naked. Then he would start out walking across the fields, through the woods, walking, walking, walking. One night about four in the morning, the sheriff of Sumter County called us up and said, "We've got one of your members in here. He's naked and we found him on the porch of a family here in town. We've got him in jail." I remember how these folks had bound this man, put handcuffs on him, and this sheriff said, "We've got him in jail and he's charged with indecent exposure."

I had many talks with this fellow. I tried to understand why he would do this, why this particular course of action when these seizures would take him. He told me this story about how he had killed a man, and as he was talking to me, I noticed his hands moving, and he became greatly emotional, and when he came to the point where he said, "And I killed that man," he began to tear at his clothes and he said, "I just wish I could *get it off my chest!*" And when he did that he popped a button and for the first time I began to catch some insight into what this man was doing. He thought that the clothing seemed to represent what society had put on him – artificiality. Society had imposed its custom upon him and had told him to go out and shoot and kill. He knew it was wrong and he just wanted to get it off; he wanted to be a naked man, made only in the image of God. He didn't want the guilt of man on him; he wanted to be free. He wanted to be forgiven. He wanted to be restored to fellowship. I think that is what he had in common with the man in the story who had been taught not to eat hog meat. This boy had been taught not to kill human flesh. Both men found themselves violating their religious upbringing and it broke them apart.

Now, I tell you, my friends, we should be very careful about what we teach our youngsters. If we are going to teach them, "Do not kill," then, for heaven's sake, let's support them in that when they get to the point where they have to face this conflict. When somebody says, "We'll put a gun in your hand and make you kill," let us support those youngsters. There is nothing that can tear a person to pieces like religious hypocrisy – teaching one thing and practicing another. It broke Judas. It well-nigh broke the man of Gadara, had it not been for the tremendous discernment of our Lord, picking this boy up, knowing what his problems were, putting him back together, sending him back home. I think our Lord is trying to pick up the broken pieces of youngsters – oh, how many of them I see on college campuses today, particularly college campuses – torn and twisted by all kinds of doctrines, unable to make sense of their early upbringing, sojourners in a foreign land, and many times deserted by the very church that mothered them. I think our Lord would say, "What is your name?" And when they say, "Legion, multitude," he says, "I can deal with your problems." And we gather around him and him alone and find, at the foot of Jesus, a face-to-face confrontation with our Lord. We find ourselves, for the first time, making sense of life and enfolded in the fellowship.

12

Things Needed for Our Peace

Four weeks after the assassination of Martin Luther King Jr. led to rioting in many American cities, Clarence Jordan spoke at Furman University.

JESUS DREW NEAR TO JERUSALEM, and when he saw the city he burst into tears over it. And he said: "If you had known, even at this time, the things that make for your peace, but now they are hidden from your eyes" (Luke 19:41–44). What were those things that could have given some peace to people of Jesus' day? I think there were four things that the people of Jesus' day needed to see that belonged to their peace but were hidden from their eyes. And I think, incidentally, these four things today are things needed for our peace and perhaps may be hidden from our own eyes.

One, these people needed a sense of national and racial humility. They were people who had been taught that they were chosen people, that they could trace their ancestry way on back to Abraham, that God had made a covenant with them, and that they were God's only people. They preached the doctrine that they were God's holy chosen people. They were looking down their noses at Gentiles and people of other races. And this kind of national and racial arrogance could but bring upon them the devastation which we today are learning comes upon people who have that kind of mind. We have seen the awful destructiveness of our own white arrogance, our own white pride, and we have not yet by any means reaped the bitter dragon seeds of the dragon's teeth which we have sown.

The storm has come and we have not yet passed through the eye of it. We have seen the destructiveness of our racial arrogance, and I think our experience on the face of this earth is demonstrating the terrible awfulness of our national arrogance. It not only will destroy us, it will keep us from being people of peace. It will also destroy other people around the world.

The second thing that these people needed to have peace that was hidden from their eyes was a realistic understanding of the nature of violence. Jesus was born in a very violent world. He was scarcely dried off before a very violent tyrant tried to kill him and murdered a bunch of little babies in his frustration. Christianity has been right in the middle of great violence and it has had something to say about how to deal with it. Now with all of the great palaver that we have had about nonviolence, Jesus did not teach nonviolence. He went further than that. He did not say that you could be nonviolent toward your enemy and win your enemy over. He would not agree with my dear friend Martin Luther King Jr. that nonviolence is a strategy by which you can accomplish your goals. It may work, it may not work. Jesus would not even attempt to use it as a strategy.

He taught something greater than that. He taught that people could be children of a God of peace and of love. He taught them to think that in the midst of evil they could face others with a love that would be unquenchable – not practical, but unquenchable. Now this may or may not accomplish its objective, but it would make men and women out of us. We would be, he said, "children of God." Children of God are not always successful. Some of them wind up on crosses like the first Christian did. Who could say that that was successful?

The next thing that I think we have to have that these people needed was a spirit of sharing. These people had gotten richer and the poor had gotten poorer and they were trying to solve their problems just like we are trying to solve ours, through taxation. They didn't have sense enough to know that you cannot solve the problem with the poor through taxation. It is the only way the government has of solving it, therefore the government can never solve it; no matter how large the war on poverty, the government cannot solve the problem of poverty. All history indicates that the higher the taxes go, the greater the division between the rich and the poor. Simple, just plain, simple arithmetic.

What if a doctor is making fifty thousand dollars a year, and paying twenty-five thousand dollars' income tax? Do you think he is going to take that out of his fifty thousand? No! He is going up on his fees enough to take in eighty thousand and he will send the government the tax. He is not going to take that tax out of his pocket. He is simply going to up his fees and pass it on to his patients. And if they are affluent enough, they will pass it on down to somebody else and they will pass it on down until finally you will get to the people on the bottom end of the pole who have nowhere to pass it and they pay with their blood and their sweat.

When their children go hungry and the rats gnaw at them and the roaches crawl all over them, they get so desperate that, since they don't have anybody to pass it down to, they start passing it back to the rich. They go to burning and looting, and we shoot them down in their tracks. The trouble with them is that they are just looting. I am not trying to advocate this for anybody, I am just saying that these folks are just trying to loot back some of the stuff that they have had looted from them. If they looted with a pistol, we put them in a penitentiary. But if they loot with a pencil, we make a deacon out of them. The real looting that goes on in this world is done in more skillful ways than with pistols and guns – that's a crude way to loot. You do it with your pencils and your figuring and it is the big boys that do the looting on the great scale who advocate that shooting down of the poor folks who are trying to pass it back.

Now, we need to understand the meaning of sharing. It isn't the matter of whether or not we are going to share with the poor. It's the matter of how you want to share or whether you are going to do it involuntarily or voluntarily. One of the things that really frightens me about a school such as this, you come here and live in this little bit of artificial heaven for four years and you think this is what the stuff the world is made out of. You drive in here and see all this flowing water, a fountain of life, and you begin looking for the great white throne – you think that you're already there. And then you get out and you think that this is a kinder world, with this beautiful landscape and its flowing fountains and its singing birds and its magnificent buildings. You think this is the kind of stuff that the world is made out of, and it simply isn't. Too many times a kid can go through four years of a school and graduate as a selfish slob, a pirate on the high seas of humanity using his silly little old degree as a weapon to exploit and crush people under him. We don't know the things that belong to our peace. We are isolated and insulated from it too frequently. We don't know the meaning of sharing.

And then lastly, I think the thing that belongs to peace is the thing that concerned Jesus most. There is a new spirit, a new mentality, something new breaking loose in people, a new attitude no longer ruled by greed and selfishness and hate and lust. A new attitude toward our roommate, a new attitude toward our professor, a new attitude toward society, a new attitude toward life. And our old values of selfishness flee away and we become ready to be poor people for Christ's sake. We don't hate the poor, we don't war on the poor! We become poor and we identify ourselves with them. You think Jesus was poor because he had to be? No, he was poor because he wanted to be. And he rode that mule not out of mockery but out of sincerity. He rode that mule into the world that is. Lowly and riding on a mule.

I challenge you to share that mentality; not to go out of this institution to lord it over your fellow human beings but to go out with a new spirit, a spirit of servant-hood, of service, and of suffering. Putting yourself at the feet of humankind and becoming poor with the poor. Not giving them a handout but handing out your *life*. From this day on my prayer is that God's spirit will break out in your heart and in my heart, that we may be new people with a new song and a new spirit living in a New Jerusalem with a new name. Around our God who said, "Behold, I make all things new."

13

The Humanity of God

In 1969, during what would be his last summer, Clarence Jordan addressed fellow pastors at the American Baptist Convention in Seattle, challenging them to see the radical implications of the incarnation, the resurrection, and the birth of the church at Pentecost. Here are some excerpts.

TODAY WHEN THE CHURCH is being attacked and challenged on every hand as a viable institution, when the church is in doubt and confused about its own identity and mission, it must make contact – it must touch base – with the rock from which it was hewn. We must look again into the faces of that crowd of witnesses which surrounds us and cheers us on in our often lonely task of being faithful witnesses to the Lord Jesus.

So I'm going back to the Book of Acts to help you drink from the spring, the refreshing waters that will give strength for the hours of heat and scorching sun, that we may be faithful witnesses in these hours that are troubling our souls and challenging our very existence. The writer, Luke, says that he has written a previous volume. He wrote the first volume to tell about all those things which Jesus got in motion, as if to infer that the second volume is to tell you about those things which Jesus *still* is getting in motion. The first volume is a biography of the life of Jesus in human flesh in one body. The second volume is the life of Jesus in his new body, the new body which Paul called the church. So the first volume is a biography of Jesus of Nazareth. The second volume is the biography of Jesus working through the church.

You will note a very close similarity between these two biographies. Both give birth narratives. In the first volume, Mary is his mother. In the second volume, the church takes the place of Mary and God implants his Holy Spirit in the church to bring forth a new kind of Son of God on the face of the earth, and it's that Son of God who is still up to his old work – preaching, teaching, and healing. So the Book of Acts is going to tell us about Jesus who has been raised from the dead, who is alive and is working now not through one body, Jesus of Nazareth, but through many bodies which make a whole – his church.

The first volume comes to a fitting climax in the ascension. Luke tells about the birth of this young fellow, how he lived and moved among us, what the reaction of the world was to him, how finally the world killed him, but how God raised him from the dead, and then the curtain falls with him going into the realm of the spirit – not up to heaven, as we are led to believe, but moving into the realm of the spirit; not leaving us here on earth, but being with us in a more real way than while he was limited to just one body.

"ALL OF THEM, including the women and Mary, Jesus' mother, and his brothers, were continually praying together" (Acts 1:12–14). The eleven disciples are there. They have been with him through all his ministry. They know what he did in volume one. They know that their task is to be volume two. They are to carry on the ministry of their Lord. But now they have somebody else with them. They have Mary, Jesus' mother, and his brothers. Mary is beginning to really become Jesus' mother.

She was told in volume one that she would give birth to a son and that son would be the Son of the Most High and that a sword would pierce her heart. She learned later that the sword that pierced her heart was the babe that was formed in her womb. And she tried to keep him. She was told that he was God's son, but the mother instinct in her wanted to keep him. She wanted him for *her* son.

When she went to the Temple with him when he was twelve years old, and he got interested in the ministerial association meeting and didn't get with them on the way back, she then came back and in a great fluster of anger said to him, "What's the matter with you? Your daddy and I have been looking for you all over everywhere and here you are at the ministerial meeting. Why did you grieve us like that?" She was saying to him, "You're my son." He was saying to her, "Yes, Mother, I am your son. But I am my Father's son also. Didn't you know that I had to be about my Father's business?"

Later on, after he had been preaching and getting himself into trouble, perhaps having been investigated by the House Un-Roman Activities Committee, and right in the shadow of the cross, his mother and his brothers come to him and I know what they want with him. They want to say, "Now look, Jesus. You're about to take this thing too far. You come on home and be a good boy. We can give you a job as foreman in the woodworking division of the carpenter shop. And I want you to forget about all of this business of being the Messiah, and all like that." I know what this mother and these brothers wanted. They wanted to keep him in the family! But Jesus' word to them was, "Who is my mother, and my brother, and my sister? Whoever does the will of my Father is my mother, and my brother, and my sister" (Matt. 12:49–50).

When we get over finally to the crucifixion, when Mary relinquished him and gave him away, gave him to humankind as God intended him to be, at last, when she lost him, she became his mother. The church, in a very real sense, gives birth to sons of God. She is the womb in which they are conceived. In my own case this was true. The little Baptist church in which I grew up nurtured me. In its womb I learned the scriptures. I suckled at its breast. And the little church thought that it not only was my mother, but also my father. And when I had to go about my Father's business, the church said, "No, son, you are piercing our hearts. We don't want to give you up." And when I finally persisted in going about my Father's business, my mother, the church, renounced me.

It is hard for a mother whose womb conceives a child of God to quit being a mother and let that child get about the Father's business. I think this is the real tension between preachers and their congregations today.

Preachers are nourished in the church. They are educated by it. They love it. It has been the umbilical cord to life for them. And yet when they get on about their Father's business, maybe getting in jail, getting in demonstrations, spending themselves to do the will of the Father, the church says, "No, child, come be my child. Stop being so much like your Father." The preacher has to say, "No, Mother, I must be about my Father's business."

I think this is the trouble of our youth today. We have been too successful with our religious education. We have finally gotten our children to catch the point! And so they get the idea that God is to be obeyed. He is to be followed. And when these kids get out with visions in their heads and dreams in their hearts and start following the very God we have nurtured within them, then we say, "No, child, be my child. Don't be so much like your Father."

At long last, though, Mary learned to be the mother of Jesus by giving him to humankind to do his Father's business. I hope and pray that before I pass on to glory, that little church that expelled me from its fellowship will realize that I really am its son, that I really do love it, and that it will gather with me and realize that you can only be a true mother of a child of God when you relinquish your motherhood and give that child to all humankind. For God did not give his Son to the church. He did not give his son to Mary. She was merely the instrument through which he came. God gave his Son to the world. And when our sons and daughters give themselves with abandon to following their Father in the lowly paths of the world, let not the church hold back and say, "Come children, be your mother's children." Let us grasp their hands, seeing in them the image of their Father, and say to them, "Sons and daughters, though it leads you to a cross, be good children of your Father."

I HAVE COMPARED the birth of the church to the birth of Jesus. We cannot understand this unless we go back and look at the Gospel of Luke and see how the first account occurred. What the virgin birth is trying to say to us is not that a man became divine, but that God Almighty took the initiative and established permanent residence on this earth! Now we, today, have reversed the virgin birth. We have reversed the incarnation. Instead of the Word becoming flesh and dwelling among us, we turn it around and we take a bit of flesh and deify it. We have deified Jesus and thus effectively rid ourselves of him even more than if we had crucified him. When God becomes a man, we don't know what to do with him. If he will just stay God, like a God ought to be, then we can deal with him. We can sing our songs to him, if he will just stay God. If he will stay in his heaven and quit coming down to this earth and dwelling among us where we have to deal with a baby in a manger and a man on the cross; if God Almighty would just stay God and quit becoming man, then we could handle him. We can build our cathedrals to him. This is the bind we get in today. We reverse the action – from heaven to earth. We turn it around and build it from earth to heaven. And salvation becomes something that we will attain someday, rather than God coming to earth to be among us. So we build our churches. We set up great monuments to God and we reject him as a human being.

A church in Georgia just set up a big twenty-five-thousand-dollar granite fountain on its lawn, circulating water to the tune of a thousand gallons a minute. Now that ought to be enough to satisfy any Baptist. But what on earth is a church taking God Almighty's money in a time of great need like this and setting up a fountain on its lawn to bubble water around? *I was thirsty . . . and ye built me a fountain.* We can handle God as long as he stays God. We can build him a fountain. But when he becomes a man, we have to give him a cup of water. So the virgin birth is simply the great transcendent truth that God Almighty has come into the affairs of man and dwelt among us.

WHEN GOD DECIDED TO ESTABLISH permanent residency upon the earth, he did not come as a foreign missionary to our shores for a brief time to bring the light to us and then return on a celestial furlough. Nor as a naturalized citizen, an alien asking for acceptance and approval conforming himself to the customs of his adopted country. But he decided to come as a native-born son, a member of the human family. That, to me, is what the virgin birth is saying – that God has decided to become a member of the human race.

So then, the virgin birth is not proof of the deity of Jesus, but rather, evidence of the humanity of God. It definitely establishes that from here on out, we cannot deal with God without confronting him in our brothers and sisters. John bears this out when he says, "And the idea, the Word, became a human being, and dwelt among us" (John 1:14).

The parable of the great judgment affirms the truth of the virgin birth: that Jesus Christ is now our brother.

He has been born here on the earth into the human family. Jesus says, "I was sick and you visited me . . . I was naked, I was hungry, I was thirsty, and I was in prison . . ." And we say, "Lord, when did we see you naked and sick and hungry and thirsty and in prison?" And Jesus says, "Inasmuch as you did it unto one of the least of these, you have done it unto me." He is affirming his membership in the human family. He is a brother. God has become one of us. The dwelling place of God is with humankind. We now can call him Immanuel, "God is with us." And we can no longer deal with God without dealing with our brothers and sisters.

John, the beloved disciple, puts it this way: "If someone says, 'I love God,' and is hating his brother, he is a phony. For the man who has no love for his physical brother cannot possibly have love for the invisible God" (1 John 4:20). So the advice we get from John is that the God-lover is also a brother-lover. Just a way of saying that from here on out, you can't have any dealings with God unless you deal with your fellow humans, for God has established residency on the earth.

YOU KNOW, on Easter Day all of us get all prettified and we get on our nice garments. We get our flowers and perfume and we talk about Jesus being raised from the dead and how he's going to take us all to heaven one of these days. If we go to the Easter sunrise services every sunrise until we die, he's going to take us to heaven when we die. Well, that might be nice, but that is not what the resurrection of Jesus is all about. God did not raise Jesus from the dead to prove that he could raise a few cantankerous saints. He could do that. Man's belief in his own immortality had been very persistent, not only in the Christian religion but outside of it. God raised Jesus from the dead for a different purpose. When Jesus came in his first body, people didn't like having God around. It was a bad place for God to be. Sort of like having a preacher in the barber shop. We felt uncomfortable with him here. So we had to get rid of him. We nailed him to the cross and said, "You go back home, God. Don't you mess around down here. We have to watch our language too much with you around. And we have to watch our ledger accounts too much when you're looking over our shoulder. And we have to be too careful on Saturday night when we're hitting the bottle rather heavy. Now you, God, you go back home where you belong and be a good God, and we'll see you at eleven o'clock on Sunday morning."

In raising Jesus from the dead, God is refusing to take our no for an answer. He is saying you can kill my boy if you wish, but I am going to raise him from the dead and put him right smack dab down there on earth again! It is God saying, I am not going to take no for an answer. I am going to raise him up, plant his feet on the earth, and put him to preaching, teaching, and healing again.

So the resurrection of Jesus was simply God's unwillingness to take our no for an answer. He raised Jesus, not as an invitation to us to come to heaven when we die, but as a declaration that he, himself, has now established permanent, eternal residence on earth. The resurrection places Jesus on this side of the grave – here and now – in the midst of this life. He is not standing on the shore of eternity beckoning us to join him there; he is standing beside us, strengthening us in this life. The good news of the resurrection of Jesus is not that we shall die and go home with him, but that he has risen and comes home with us, bringing with him all his hungry, naked, thirsty, sick, prisoner brothers and sisters with him.

And we say, "Jesus, we'd be glad to have you, but all these motley brothers and sisters of yours, you had better send them home. You come in and we'll have some fried chicken. But you get your sick, naked, cold brothers and sisters out of here. I don't want them getting my new rug all messed up which I just got through vacuuming."

The resurrection is simply God's way of saying, "You might reject me if you will, but I am going to have the last word. I am going to put my son right down there in the midst of you and he is going to dwell among you from here on out."

So on the morning of the resurrection, God put life in the present tense, not in the future. He gave us not a promise, but a presence. Not a hope for the future, but power for the present. Not so much the assurance that we shall live someday, but that he is risen today. Jesus' resurrection is not to convince the incredulous, nor to reassure the fearful, but to enkindle the believers. The proof that God raised Jesus from the dead is not the empty tomb, but the full hearts of his transformed disciples. The crowning evidence that he lives is not a vacant grave, but a Spirit-filled fellowship. Not a rolled-away stone, but a carried-away church. We are the evidence of the resurrection. Look at what he has done to us and is doing through us.

Sources

Who Was Clarence Jordan?

This brief biographical sketch is drawn from the definitive biography, *Clarence Jordan: A Radical Pilgrimage in Scorn of the Consequences* (Mercer University Press, 2017), by Frederick L. Downing, professor of philosophy and religious studies at Valdosta State University, who also selected the readings in this volume. See that biography for full annotation of primary sources.

1. Impractical Christianity

"Impractical Christianity," *Sunday School Young People's Quarterly* (Nashville, TN: Sunday School Board of the Southern Baptist Convention, 1948). Located at the Southern Baptist Historical Library and Archive, Nashville, TN.

2. The Meaning of Christian Fellowship

"The Meaning of Christian Fellowship," *Prophetic Religion: A Journal of Christian Faith and Action* 7:1 (Spring 1946), 3-6, 26.

3. What Is the Word of God?

From "The Church and the Bible," a sermon, Baptist Church, Brookings, South Dakota, December 3, 1952. Located in the Clarence Jordan Collection, Hargrett Rare Book and Manuscript Library, University of Georgia, MS 2340, B 29, F 12.

4. White Southern Christians and Race

"Racial Frontiers," *Baptist Student* (November 1941), 6-7. Located at the Southern Baptist Historical Library and Archive, Nashville, TN.

5. No Promised Land without the Wilderness

From "A People, Its Leader, and Its God: The Life and Work of Moses," a lecture, St. Paul's Evangelical and Reformed Church, November 22, 1955. Located in the Clarence Jordan Collection, Hargrett Rare Book and Manuscript Library, University of Georgia, MS 2340, B 30, F 3.

6. The Ten Commandments

From "The Ten Commandments," a sermon, Goshen College, Goshen Indiana, May 28, 1965. Located in the Clarence Jordan Collection, Hargrett Rare Book and Manuscript Library, University of Georgia, MS 2340, B 7, F 13.

7. Jesus, Leader of the Poor

From "Jesus the Rebel," a sermon, Goshen College, February 9, 1965. Located in the Clarence Jordan Collection, Hargrett Rare Book and Manuscript Library, University of Georgia, MS 2340, B 4, F 2.

8. Love Your Enemies

From "Loving your Enemies," a sermon, Goshen College, February 8, 1965. Located in the Clarence Jordan Collection, Hargrett Rare Book and Manuscript Library, University of Georgia, MS 2340, B 4, F 1.

9. Jesus and Possessions

From "Jesus and Possessions," a sermon, Goshen College, February 10, 1965. Located in the Clarence Jordan Collection, Hargrett Rare Book and Manuscript Library, University of Georgia, MS 2340, B 4, F 3.

10. Metamorphosis

From "Metamorphosis," a sermon, Goshen College, February 11, 1965. Located in the Clarence Jordan Collection, Hargrett Rare Book and Manuscript Library, University of Georgia, MS 2340, B 4, F 4.

11. The Man from Gadara

From "Man from Gadara," a sermon, Goshen College, February 11, 1965. Located in the Clarence Jordan Collection, Hargrett Rare Book and Manuscript Library, University of Georgia, MS 2340, B 4, F 5.

12. Things Needed for Our Peace

From "Things Needed for Our Peace," a sermon, Furman University, Greenville, South Carolina, May 1, 1968. Located in the Special Collections and Archives, Furman University.

13. The Humanity of God

From "Incarnational Evangelism," a sermon, The American Baptist Convention, Seattle, Washington, May 1969. Located in the Clarence Jordan Collection, Hargrett Rare Book and Manuscript Library, University of Georgia, MS 2340, B 7, F 2. This and several other sermons excerpted here are published in full in *The Substance of Faith: And Other Cotton Patch Sermons,* by Clarence Jordan, edited by Dallas Lee (New York: Association Press, 1972).

Plough Spiritual Guides

The Reckless Way of Love
Notes on Following Jesus
Dorothy Day

Love in the Void
Where God Finds Us
Simone Weil

The Prayer God Answers
Eberhard Arnold and Richard J. Foster

Why We Live in Community
Eberhard Arnold and Thomas Merton

The Scandal of Redemption
When God Liberates the Poor, Saves Sinners, and Heals Nations
Oscar Romero

That Way and No Other
Following God through Storm and Drought
Amy Carmichael

Thunder in the Soul
To Be Known by God
Abraham Joshua Heschel

Plough Publishing House
845-572-3455 ◆ info@plough.com
PO BOX 398, Walden, NY 12586, USA
Robertsbridge, East Sussex TN32 5DR, UK
4188 Gwydir Highway, Elsmore, NSW 2360, Australia
www.plough.com